Edited by
William W. Denlinger and R. Annabel Rathman

Cover design by
Bob Groves

the Chinese
Shar-Pei

DENLINGER'S PUBLISHERS, LTD.
Box 76, Fairfax, Virginia 22030

by
Paul D. Strang
Eve C. Olsen

Chi-Tzu of Foo. Bred by Mrs. Victor Seas. Owned by Jane Zintak, Rome, Italy.

Library of Congress Cataloging in Publication Data
Strang, Paul D
    The Chinese Shar-Pei.
    1. Chinese Shar-Pei. I. Olsen, Eve C., joint author.
II. Title.
SF429.C48S77   636.7'2   79-55675
ISBN 0-87714-072-3

Foreword

Down-Homes Little Pea, a pregnant, two-year-old Shar-Pei bitch, came to our house from Matgo Law's kennels in Hong Kong in October 1973. Just a month after she arrived she presented us with the first U. S.-whelped litter of Matgo's own breeding.

Today, six years and three litters later, she has become our "Honorable Grandmother," but she still collects quite a crowd of fascinated spectators whenever we appear in public together.

Answering the inevitable questions about the breed is easier today than it was back in 1973. At that time there was no literature on these dogs and most of our knowledge had to come from slowly acquired practical experience. Actually, the lack of a Shar-Pei breed book has been a real handicap to all fanciers from the very beginning.

But now, at last, we have a book that surpasses all our hopes and expectations. This work by Paul Strang and Eve Olsen will be eagerly studied not only by those interested in the Shar-Pei but also by the owners of many other breeds as well.

With the true distinction of impartial historians, observers, and critics, the authors take us, step by step, from the earliest days in China right up to the present time. Their enthusiasm is infectious as they cover early breeders, bloodlines, pedigrees, care and feeding, mating, whelping, and showing, and then end up with a ringing salute to the future.

May both the Chinese Shar-Pei and its two champions, Paul Strang and Eve Olsen, be around for a long time to come!

Lois E. Alexander

Acknowledgments

We are grateful to the many Shar-Pei owners who provided information on their dogs and permitted us to include photos of their Shar-Pei in this book. Unfortunately, space is not available to list all who gave us encouragement and special assistance, but we wish particularly to thank Mr. Ernest W. Albright and Mrs. Ruth Fink for the exhaustive and detailed information they provided; Mr. Frank Ferris for the data on early registrations of Chinese Fighting Dogs with the American Dog Breeders Association; Ms. Gloria Bilotta for the illustrations of correct and incorrect conformation included here; Mr. Edwin Tennyson for his photography; and The Original Chinese Shar-Pei Club of America, Inc., The Chinese Shar-Pei Club of America, Inc. (East Coast), and The Southern California Chinese Shar-Pei Club for the data on club activities as well as the membership information they permitted us to include here.

Without the cooperation of these many dedicated admirers of the breed, we should never have been able to compile this work.

It is our fervent hope that this volume will prove valuable to all Shar-Pei fanciers—those of the present and those of the future—as a showcase of the breed as it appears today.

Paul D. Strang
and
Eve C. Olsen

Left, Paul Strang with Chinese Shar-Pei in Macao.

Below, Eve Olsen with Willowledge puppy.

Tennyson

Contents

Mo-Chu, owned by Kenneth Halbert, Saint Joseph, Missouri.

Shar-Pei puppy at Ohio Rare Breed Club Show, 1977.

Left, Down-Homes The Unicorn (dog), and right, Down-Homes Ugo (bitch), both by Down-Homes Clown-Nosed Buddha ex Down-Homes Fleur, and whelped in Hong Kong November 21, 1978. In center, Down-Homes Von Kar (bitch), by Down-Homes Prince of Darkness ex Down-Homes Quinn Anne III, whelped in Hong Kong November 23, 1978. All bred by Matgo Law and all owned by Larry and Shirley Rafferty, Eagle Creek, Oregon.

Meet the Chinese Shar-Pei

In the Chinese language there are no plural forms for words, so whether one is referring to a single dog of the breed or to several, the spelling is the same—*Shar-Pei*. And in Chinese, the name of the breed is pronounced *Sah-Pay*.

The Chinese Shar-Pei is listed in the 1978 *Guinness Book of World Records* as the world's rarest dog. Be that as it may, the Shar-Pei is certainly one of the world's most extraordinary dogs, and this comical fellow, dubbed Mr. Wrinkles by the popular press, has so captivated the hearts of admirers in the United States and Europe that dog lovers are traveling around the world to seek him out.

The story of the Shar-Pei's climb from near oblivion to international stardom is an intriguing one. Having survived for over two thousand years as a valued member of the Chinese family, the breed had reached such a low ebb in 1971 that only a few scattered specimens were known to exist. Now it seems likely that this amiable, medium-sized, amusingly wrinkled dog is about to break all records for a comeback.

The fact that the Shar-Pei is thriving and growing in fame and popularity is no doubt due in part to the affection we automatically feel for an "endangered species" and in part to the breed's unusual appearance. But most of all, people are falling in love with the dog because he is a highly intriguing animal, bringing something of the fun and glamour of the circus into our lives.

Certainly no other breed presents such a startling appearance. The head is deeply furrowed, and the back and sides are more or less pleated with loose skin which often extends down the legs, giving a droopy-drawers effect on the hindquarters—or that of oversize pantyhose.

Puppies are even more wrinkled than adults and appear to be absolutely engulfed in a coat many sizes too large for their pudgy frames. Even as an adult this fellow's superabundance of skin forms deep folds when he is seated. Like a raggedy clown, the Shar-Pei is both hilarious and irresistible.

Viewed from the front, the head of the Shar-Pei reminds one of a hippopotamus. The face appears almost flat, with little or no stop from the skull to the broad, blunt muzzle. Small ears (but not cropped) and widely set, dark, deeply set eyes complete the picture.

In size the Shar-Pei is about equal to a strongly built Bull Terrier. The body is short-coupled and well-balanced, with a broad, deep chest giving the dog a strong, solid, square appearance.

Usual colors are light or deep fawn, cream, or black. An unusual feature of the coat is that it should not be slick or glossy, and, in fact, should have a somewhat gritty feel because of its stiff and bristly texture. The name Shar-Pei means "sandy coat" and refers to this point.

The tongue of the Shar-Pei is bluish-black, similar to that of the Chow Chow. For this reason some fanciers see a rather close relationship between the two breeds. Other fanciers, pointing to his close association with the combat ring, think the Shar-Pei may be an Oriental variety of Bulldog. But most fanciers consider the Shar-Pei as unique, endowed with qualities and attributes that set him apart from all other breeds.

Formerly the Shar-Pei was sometimes trained for dog fights and in this role became known as the Chinese Fighting Dog. But those days are now behind him and the ease with which he accepts his present position as companion, pet, and protector leads us to believe he must usually have been drugged (or tormented) before engaging in combat.

On first encountering one of these rare dogs, people are invariably astounded, amused, and intrigued by his unusual appearance. Recovering from their initial shock, they immediately want to know more. "What is he really like beneath all those wrinkles?" they ask.

His gentlemanly nature, of course, stands out. Two thousand years of Oriental heritage and environment have endowed him with the ability to meet any and all situations in a calm and unruffled manner. With neurotic behavior seemingly on the increase in a number of our better known breeds, the Shar-Pei's reliable conduct is certainly a big plus in his favor.

The Shar-Pei was bred for intelligence in a rather informal manner. If an individual dog did not show a high degree of intelligence, he was

Ch. Arno, imported Neapolitan Mastiff owned by Michael A. Sottile, Bridgewater, New Jersey. The Neapolitan Mastiff is believed to be one of the breeds which figured prominently in the ancestral lines of the Chinese Shar-Pei.

slaughtered and eaten. Such pragmatic practices are understandable when we remember the degree of poverty in which the Chinese peasant lived for centuries.

Being sturdy, compact, active, and intelligent, the Shar-Pei is perfectly suited to city, suburban, or country living. The short-haired coat is easy to keep clean, and a big plus lies in the fact that the Shar-Pei coat does not shed. The dog is outgoing by nature and just as happy indoors as out.

The Shar-Pei loves to ride in a car, is easily trained, and is not a barker. Furthermore, anyone who has had experience with some of the breeds that love to wander and stray (often winding up miles away from home) will appreciate the fact that the Shar-Pei is a strict homebody. He much prefers his own realm to the grass on the other side of the fence.

Because of his stay-at-home nature and his deep loyalty to family and friends, the Shar-Pei makes a natural watchdog. Being both calm and obedient, he does not tend to overreact. He is active and compact, with firm stature.

Although not yet accepted for registration by The American Kennel Club, it is only a matter of time before the Shar-Pei achieves this official recognition. And after that the final accolade will come on the day a Best-in-Show award is handed to Mr. Wrinkles, the Chinese Shar-Pei.

Robert Chan's kennel in Hong Kong.

Origin and Early History

Differences of opinion or lack of concrete evidence often complicates the history of the origin and development of some of our breeds. But in the case of the Chinese Shar-Pei no such problems occur; everyone agrees that the Shar-Pei has existed for centuries in the southern provinces of his native land bordering on the South China Sea.

Over two thousand years ago this was the all-purpose, general utility dog kept by the peasant-farmers of the area. The Shar-Pei was used for hunting such animals as the wild boar or to protect the livestock from predators, but most of all he served as guardian of his master's home. He was selectively bred for intelligence, for strength, and for the valued "warrior scowl" that would increase his menacing appearance and help to intimidate the barbarian thieves, against whom the farmers were always at war.

During the Han Dynasty (202 B.C.–A.D. 220), artistic fired-clay statues and statuettes depicting the life of the era were very popular, and the dog was a favorite subject. Fortunately, many of these Han statuettes have survived to this day and may be seen in such places as the Louvre and the British Museum. One such statuette is on display in the Asian Art Museum in San Francisco, Avery Brundage Collection, as the "Chinese Tomb Dog." And there are others in private collections. Anyone who harbors a tendency to doubt the antiquity of the Shar-Pei has but to examine the Han dog figurines. These dogs portray, unmistakably, the same breed we know today. Although then not quite so wrinkled as now, the rugged, foursquare look, the tail wheeled over the back, and the celebrated warrior scowl are lifelike to an amazing degree.

It is interesting to note that the time of the Han Dynasty in China corresponds rather closely to the time of the Roman Empire in Europe. Under the Romans, European dogs were often trained as fighters, matched either against others of their kind or against bears and lions. But in China there is no record of the dogs of the Han Dynasty ever being used in such fashion. Jean Yu, Orientalist of Washington, D. C., has researched ancient Chinese manuscripts and insists that the Shar-Pei's original purpose was for use as hunting dogs and that their principal quarry was the mongoose.

Nevertheless, because of their strength and appearance, these dogs were introduced to a combat role at a later time in history.

The village of Dah Let, in Southern China's Kwangtung Province near Canton, was at one time known as a gambler's haven. Betting on dog fights was a popular pastime and the Han dog became a favorite contestant.

Dah Let dog breeders, anxious to improve the breed's ability and its chances in the ring, set out to perfect some of the main characteristics we know today. The bristly coat was developed to make it distasteful in an opponent's mouth; the very loose skin to enable a dog to turn and twist in the grasp of his opponent, making it difficult for the enemy to get to the Shar-Pei's flesh; and the recurved canine teeth to provide a hook-like hold on the antagonist. He possessed stamina and determination, but before a battle, the canine contender was given wine and stimulating drugs to heighten his aggressiveness.

But while these developments were taking place in our breed, other fight promoters and gamblers were proceeding along a different line. Mastiffs, Bulldogs, and other breeds were brought to China from the West, crossbred, and selected for vicious temperament. The native fighting Han dog of Dah Let proved to be no match for these bigger, stronger, more ferocious dogs. No longer in demand, their breeding was neglected and the numbers of the Dah Let fighting dogs rapidly decreased.

But what was to be the near fatal blow to the breed occurred when the Chinese Communists came to power. One of their first moves was to impose such a heavy tax on dogs that only the extremely wealthy could afford the luxury of canine companionship. And then a further edict declared dogs a "decadent bourgeois luxury" and banned dog breeding. In 1947 the tax on dogs that still survived was sharply increased.

As a result of all this Communist Party pressure, by 1950 only scattered specimens of the noble dog of the Han Dynasty were left. From isolated South China villages, fanciers in Macao (Portuguese China) and Hong Kong were able to secure an occasional specimen, but the breed was on the brink of being lost forever.

Above, five-month-old Shar-Pei from Southern China. A gift from the Peoples Republic of China to Mr. William Morrison.

Above, Dr. Robert Brown's Ning Po (from Hong Kong) at three months. Breeder, Matgo Law.

Above, Down-Homes Jade Ying, bred by Matgo Law and owned by Pat Pagnard, Morral, Ohio.

Above, Albrights Ho Wun Wu Ti Of Han, bred by Ernest Albright and owned by Jack and Jan Grady, Roswell, Georgia.

Below, Wind Rush Shami-Jade (bitch) at seven months. Owned by Barbara Cogburn, Wind Rush Kennel, Moore, Oklahoma.

Below, Wind Rush Twi-Linn (male) at seven months. Litter mate of Shami-Jade and also owned by Barbara Cogburn, Wind Rush Kennel, Moore, Oklahoma.

The Rescue Operation

Just how close the Shar-Pei came to losing the battle for survival is shown by the fact that the May 1971 issue of the magazine *Dogs,* published in New York, carried an article on rare breeds and printed a picture of a Shar-Pei, describing it as "possibly the last surviving specimen of the breed."

The story was very nearly accurate, and if a copy of the magazine had not accidentally come into the hands of Mr. Matgo Law, a young and energetic Hong Kong dog fancier, the Shar-Pei might well have passed into history without further notice.

But Matgo Law, it turns out, owned several of these dogs and with another fancier, Mr. Chung Ching Ming, had already conceived the idea of a rescue operation to prevent the breed from being lost forever. These two fanciers feared that Hong Kong might some day become a part of The People's Republic of China and that the wholesale destruction of dogs that had occurred in China would be repeated in Hong Kong. The odds seemed hopeless, but reading the article gave Mr. Law an idea.

With the typical Hong Kong flair for intelligent planning and superior execution, Matgo Law composed a letter to Marjorie Farnsworth, Editor of *Dogs.* In his letter Mr. Law outlined his plans, enclosed pictures of the few dogs he and Mr. Chung Ching Ming had been able to discover from their diligent search of the area, and ended with a plea for help and cooperation from interested American fanciers.

Publication of his letter and pictures in the April 1973 issue of *Dogs* rocketed the Shar-Pei from obscurity and possible oblivion to instant star-status and fame. Over two hundred letters poured in, many from buyers anxious to procure puppies or breeding stock. But because the entire number of dogs known to exist at that time totaled only a dozen or so individuals, it was some months before any sales could be made.

Nevertheless, American enthusiasts did eventually begin to receive a trickle of puppies from Matgo Law and also managed to discover a few more isolated dogs in Macao and Taiwan. Within a couple of years of the Shar-Pei's premature obituary, kennels had been established in California, Oregon, Ohio, Indiana, North Carolina, Virginia, and Pennsylvania.

Pictures of American-bred Shar-Pei have now appeared in over six hundred newspapers and magazines, both in this country and around the world. The demand for American-bred puppies is constantly increasing and is being met by litters from the original imports plus a continuing stream of new imports from Hong Kong. Mr. Law hopes that one day the Shar-Pei will be as popular in the United States as are the Pekingese and the Chow Chow, both of which also originated in China.

American Shar-Pei clubs have been formed and are actively engaged in furthering the interests of the breed. American breeders have already produced a number of dogs of exceptional quality and it seems evident that the remarkable dog of the Han Dynasty is on his way to establishing a new dynasty of his own.

However, in order to assume his rightful position of eminence on the American scene, the Shar-Pei must secure the status of a duly recognized breed from The American Kennel Club. And this is a rather formidable task, for the AKC rules and regulations are very strict indeed.

First of all, a Standard, which provides a detailed measure for qualitative evaluation of the breed's individuals, must be agreed upon. Further, the breed must be represented by at least 650 specimens possessing five-generation pedigrees—and these dogs must represent a broad geographical distribution throughout the country. It is vitally important that as many dogs as possible be registered.

It is obvious that to achieve the goal of AKC recognition, all breeders and owners must keep meticulous records on all phases of breed history, on dogs imported and exported, on pedigrees, and on all litters whelped.

Above, Ro-Gean's Kim of Wyloway at five months. Bred by Kensel and Ruth Fink and co-owned by Simone Demirjian and Charles Murphy, Jr.

Above, left, Fawn (bitch) and right, Ro Ro II (male), both six months of age. Owner, Ernest W. Albright. Photo by Jayne Langdon.

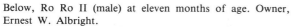

Below, Ro Ro II (male) at eleven months of age. Owner, Ernest W. Albright.

Above, Ming Yun (bitch) at fourteen months. Owned by Ernest W. Albright. Photo by Jayne Langdon.

Above, Ting, bitch, at four months. Owner, Ernest W. Albright.

Below, Ting (bitch) at fifteen months. Owner, Ernest W. Albright.

The Standards

At the present time Shar-Pei breeders in the United States look for guidance as to points of the breed to three slightly different Standards.

The first, called the Chinese Standard, is translated from the one which was drawn up by the Hong Kong and Kowloon Kennel Association and is currently used in China.

The second was drawn up by members of The Original Chinese Shar-Pei Club of America, Inc. The third is the Official Standard of The Chinese Shar-Pei Club of America, Inc. (East Coast). For the most part, these latter two are simplified and clarified versions of the Chinese Standard. But both relax to some degree the details regarding the tail and the coat beyond the provisions of the Chinese Standard. These changes were made, primarily, to allow breeders in this country to take full advantage of the genetic pool carried by all the imported dogs.

For the benefit of those who are interested in the complete picture, we give here these three Standards.

Above, Fawn, year old bitch. Owned by Ernest W. Albright.

Above and below, Chi-Tzu of Foo. Bred by Mrs. Victor Seas and owned by Jane Zintak, Rome, Italy.

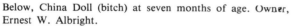

Below, China Doll (bitch) at seven months of age. Owner, Ernest W. Albright.

THE CHINESE STANDARD

Origin and Characteristics

This is a real Chinese breed that has existed for centuries in the provinces near the South China Sea. Its original home is believed to be the village of "Dah Let" in the Kwangtung Province. Lacking other entertainment, the farmers and villagers of the area staged contests between their dogs. In time the breed developed all the features of a gladiator which will be mentioned specifically, point by point, in the following structural description.

One very particular feature of the breed is the bluish-black tongue which is also a feature of the Chow Chow. Both, too, possess a somewhat similar dignified expression and both have an excellent guarding instinct. However, the Shar-Pei is by no means a smooth-coated Chow. One of these two breeds may be descended from the other or they may both share a common ancestor.

In character the Shar-Pei has a sweet disposition and only fights if taught to do so by his master from infancy. Instead, he is a well-balanced dog with a dignified, though scowling, expression. He is loyal to the death towards his family but aloof towards strangers. He is a natural household guardian and housebreaks himself as a very young puppy.

General Appearance

An active, compact, short-coupled dog well-knit in frame with a firm, determined, foursquare stance giving him the appearance of a severe warrior.

Head and Skull

Skull flat and broad, rather large in proportion to the body, with little stop. Profuse and fine wrinkles are found on the forehead and cheeks and continue on to form the heavy dewlaps. The muzzle is moderately long and broad from the eyes to the end of the nose, without any suggestion of tapering but rather resembling the mouth-shape of a hippopotamus.

Nose

Black, large and wide. Occasionally there are cream dogs with a light-colored nose and light-fawn dogs with a self-colored nose, but a black nose is preferable.

Eyes

Dark, small, almond-shaped and sunken. A light color may be found in cream and light fawn dogs. The sunken, small eyes are an advantage in a contest as they reduce chances of injury to the eye. Also the sunken eyes and wrinkles on the forehead help give the typical scowling expression of the breed.

Mouth

Teeth strong and level, with a scissors bite. The canines are recurved (increasing the difficulty for an opponent to free himself from their grip). Tongue bluish-black. Flews and the roof of the mouth black. Gums preferably black.

Ears

Small, rather thick, equilaterally triangular in shape and slightly rounded at the tip, set well forward over the eyes and wide apart. In contrast to the Chow the ears should set tightly to the skull and be as small as possible. This minimizes the opportunity for an opponent to get a grip on the ears. Some Shar-Pei have ears as small as a human's thumbnail; just covering the inside of the ear.

Neck

Strong, full, set well on the shoulders with heavy skin-folds and abundant dewlap.

Forequarters

Shoulders muscular and sloping. Forelegs straight, of moderate length and with good bone.

Body

Chest broad and deep, back short; the lowest part of the backline is just behind the withers and rises to the loin. The backline is similar to that of the Bulldog, yet not so pronounced as the latter.

Echoing the wrinkles on the head and the dewlap there is a lot of folding skin on the body. This abundant loose skin allows a contestant to turn and attack even though a certain part of his body is gripped by the opponent.

Hindquarters

Hindlegs muscular and strong. Hocks slightly bent and well let down; giving length and strength from loin to hock. (The hind legs are not as straight as those of the Chow.)

Feet

Moderate in size, compact and strong. Toes well defined, with high knuckles, giving a firm stance.

Tail

Thick and round at the base, then evenly tapering to a fine point. The three types of tail carriage are described as follows, in order of merit. The most desirable is a tight curl, falling to either side. Sometimes the curl is so tight as to resemble a large ancient Chinese coin. The second type is curled in a loose ring. In the third type of carriage the tail curves over towards, but does not touch,

Right, Shimo (bitch) whelped April 1, 1979. Bred and owned by Ernest W. and Madeline Albright, Pleasant Hill, California.

Left, China Soule, four-year-old male, and Ming Yun, three-year-old bitch.

Right, Down-Homes Ip-Win-Sun, whelped February 25, 1976. By Down-Homes Clown-Nosed Buddha ex Down-Homes Anne Revival. Breeder, Matgo Law. Owner, Roma J. Baker.

the back. This last style seems to emphasize the wiggle of a happy, eager, playful dog.

On any type of tail carriage the tail should be set high up on the loin and distinctly display the anus. (A coward tucks his tail between his legs. The demand for a tightly curled tail is obvious.)

Coat

Another peculiar feature of the breed, as it is quite harsh to the touch and stands out at a 90 degree angle from the skin. Due to its bristly nature it would be most uncomfortable when held in an opponent's mouth.

The short (horse) coat is extremely short, shorter even than the Bulldogs'—a similar coat is deemed too long.

The long (brush) coat varies somewhat in length but should be as stiff as a hairbrush. There is no undercoat in either variety. Neither coat should be shining or lustrous but neither should it appear to be unhealthy.

Color

Whole colors—black, deep-fawn, light-fawn and cream, frequently shaded, the underpart of the tail and the backs of the thighs being a lighter color, but not in patches or parti-colored.

Weight and Size

About 18–20 inches at the shoulder; weight 40–50 lbs. The dog is heavier than the bitch and more squarely built. It is important that the individuals should be well-balanced.

Faults

Spotted tongue.

Tail carried horizontally (as in the Bull Terrier) or lowered, covering the anus.

A flat, long, shining coat—not harsh and off-standing.

Tapering muzzle like a fox—not blunt enough.

Sylvanna Chan with puppies in Hong Kong.

Ro-Gean's Foo-Men Gow (Fazoo). By Down-Homes Jade Ming ex Albrights Loo Mang. Owner, Rhea A. Bartha, Lookout Mountain, Tennessee.

OFFICIAL STANDARD OF THE ORIGINAL CHINESE SHAR-PEI CLUB OF AMERICA

Note: The fourth organizational meeting of The Original Chinese Shar-Pei Club of America, Inc., was held on February 22, 1976, at Pleasant Hill, California. At this meeting, the members present, noting the great variety in the type of Shar-Pei, composed the "Official Standard of the Chinese Shar-Pei Club of America." This document was voted on and passed. The consensus was that this Standard be revised only after a five-year period had elapsed (1981), since it takes at least five generations to eliminate faults or standardize a breed. It is this Official Standard of The Original Chinese Shar-Pei Club of America, sent to the members in February 1979, which follows.

General Appearance

1. An active, compact, short coupled dog, well knit in frame, giving a square build, standing firm on the ground with a calm and firm stature.
2. The gait is a free, balanced and vigorous single track.

Head and Skull

3. Flat and broad, rather large in proportion with the body, with little stop.
4. Profuse and fine wrinkles appear upon the forehead and cheek and continue to form heavy dewlaps.
5. Muzzle moderately long and broad from the eyes to the point of the nose (without any suggestion of tapering, but rather in the mouth-shape of a hippopotamus).

Nose

6. Black, large and wide. Occasionally there are cream dogs with light colored noses, fawn with brick noses, but a black nose is preferable.

Eyes

7. Dark, small, almond-shaped and sunken (a light color is sometimes found in cream and light fawn dogs).
8. The sunken small eyes are advantageous to reduce chances of injury to the eyes.
9. Also sunken eyes and wrinkles upon the forehead help the scowling expression of the breed.

Mouth

10. Teeth strong and level, giving scissor bite; the canines somewhat curved.
11. Tongue bluish-black. A bluish-black tongue is preferable. Pink and spotted (or flowered) are allowable.
12. Flews, roof of mouth and gums preferably black. Light colors found in cream and light fawn dogs.

Ears

13. Small, rather thick, equilateral triangular in shape and slightly rounded at the tip, set well forward over the eyes and wide apart.
14. The ears should be set as tightly to the skull as possible and be small.

Neck

15. Strong, full, set well on the shoulders with heavy folding skin and abundant dewlaps.

Forequarters

16. Shoulders muscular and sloping.
17. Forelegs straight and moderate length with good bones.

Body

18. Chest broad and deep, back short, the lowest part of the body line is just behind the withers and rises to the loin.
19. The top line is level with a slight arch over the loin.
20. The abundant loose skin is a characteristic feature of the breed.

Hindquarters

21. Hindquarters muscular and strong; short hocks.

Feet

22. Moderate in size, compact and firmly set; toes well split up with high knuckles, giving a firm stand.
23. Hind dew-claws should be removed at birth.

Tail

24. Any type. The base should be high up on the loin, showing the anus. A dog with no tail is not disqualified.

Coat

25. Another distinctive feature of the breed. The coat is extremely short and bristly, and harsh to touch.
26. It is not slick and glossy, but by no means gives the impression of an unhealthy coat.

Color

27. Solid colors—black, light or dark shades of fawn, and cream.
28. Frequently shaded on tail and back of thighs, a lighter color; but not in patches or two colors.

Weight and Size

29. Around 18–20 inches at withers.
30. Around 35–50 lbs.
31. Dog is heavier than bitch and more square built.
32. Dog should appear well proportioned.

Above, Albright's Ho Hsiung at one year and one month. Owner, Walter "Dugan" Skinner, Wolcottville, Indiana.

Above, Shar-Pei owned by Linda B. Murphy, Toledo, Ohio.

Below, Foo-Z (brush coat bitch) at four and a half months. Owners, Mr. and Mrs. Walter "Dugan" Skinner, Wolcottville, Indiana.

Below, one and a half month old Shar-Pei from Chinese Diamond Kennels.

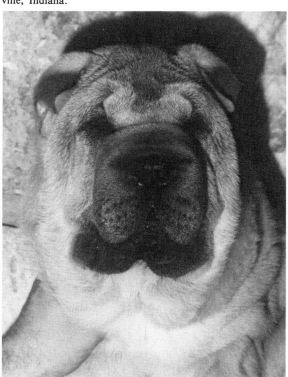

OFFICIAL STANDARD OF THE CHINESE SHAR-PEI CLUB OF AMERICA, INC.

General Appearance:

The Chinese Shar-Pei is an active, short coupled dog, well-knit in frame, giving a square build, standing firm on the ground with a calm and firm stature. The wrinkled head must be carried proudly and the whole demeanor should be one of poise and alertness.

Head and Skull:

The skull is flat and broad, rather large in proportion with the body, with little stop. Profuse and fine wrinkles appear upon the forehead and cheek and continue to form heavy dewlaps. Muzzle moderately long and broad from the eyes to the point of nose (without any suggestion of tapering—not like a fox, but rather in the mouth-shape of a hippopotamus).

Nose:

Black, large and wide is greatly desired. Occasionally there are cream dogs with light-colored noses, fawn with brick noses. A pink or pinkish tinge should not penalize an otherwise first-class specimen.

Eyes:

Dark, almond-shaped and sunken. Dark eyes are preferred, but a light color is sometimes found in cream and light fawn dogs. Bi-colored eyes are a definite disqualification. The small sunken eyes are advantageous in reducing injury to the eyes. Also, the sunken eyes and wrinkles upon the forehead help the scowling expression of the breed.

Mouth:

Teeth strong and level, giving scissors bite; the canines somewhat curved. A bluish-black tongue is preferable; flowered (spotted) is acceptable; a pink tongue is a flaw, but should not penalize an otherwise first-class specimen. Flews, roof of mouth, and gums preferably black. Light colors found in cream and light fawn dogs acceptable and not a disqualification.

Ears:

Small, thick, triangular in shape and slightly rounded at the tip, set well forward over the eyes and wide apart. The ears should be small and set tightly to the skull. Erect, bat-type ears (like a French Bulldog) are a definite disqualification.

Neck:

Strong, full, set well on the shoulders with heavy folding skin and abundant dewlaps.

Forequarters:

Shoulders muscular and sloping. Forelegs straight or slightly turned out and moderate length with good bones.

Hindquarters:

Hindquarters muscular and strong; second thigh well-developed; short hocks.

Body:

Chest broad and deep, back short, loins short and broad. The top line is level with a slight rise over the loin. The abundant loose skin is a characteristic feature of the breed.

Feet moderate in size, compact and firmly set; toes well split up with high knuckles, giving a firm stand.

Hind dew-claws, if any, should be removed.

Tail. Any type. Should be set high on top line, showing the anus.

Coat:

Three types of coat: a. short, bristly; b. short soft; c. long soft.

Each to be judged individually and are not to compete against each other except for best of breed.

Under no circumstances are judges to show personal preferences to coat alone.

Color:

Solid colors—black and shades of black; red and shades of red; fawn and shades of fawn (including cream).

Frequently shaded on tail and back of thighs; a lighter color, but not in patches of two colors.

Patches of two (2) colors on skin or coat are considered a disqualification.

Gait:

The gait is a free, balanced and vigorous single track.

Weight and Size:

Around 18–22 inches at withers. Weight 35–60 pounds. Dog is heavier and more muscular than the bitch. All dogs and bitches should appear well-proportioned and well-balanced.

Fault

1. Fox-like muzzle—Severe Fault
2. Overshot or undershot jaw—Severe Fault
3. Eyes too large and prominent—Severe Fault
4. Pink Tongue—Sometimes a Slight Fault

Disqualification

1. Two-toned eyes.
2. Bat-type ears.
3. Parti-colored skin or coat.
4. Temperament—overaggressive or vicious.

Above, Down-Homes "Pea" litter at five weeks. Three dogs and five bitches (blacks, reds, and fawns), all raised. Sired by Down-Homes King Kong ex Down-Homes Fleur.

Above, Down-Homes Clown-Nosed Buddha (standing) and Down-Homes Harmony (on bench). Photo taken at a dog show in 1975. Buddha is a heavy-boned cream dog with a top show record in Hong Kong.

Above, Down-Homes Little Pea (bitch) whelped in Hong Kong on November 17, 1971. By Down-Homes Sweet Pea ex Down-Homes Anne Revival. Little Pea was exported in whelp in 1972 to Lois E. Alexander, San Luis Obispo, California.

Down-Homes Oriental Pearl, lovely fawn bitch, at five weeks of age. Exported from Hong Kong to Ellen Weathers, San Juan Capistrano, California.

Below, Down-Homes Mui Chu. This lovely bitch was whelped in Macao in 1971 and exported to Ernest W. Albright in 1973. She died in January 1976.

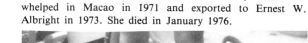

Below, Matgo and Harine Law at home, November 1977, with Down-Homes Clown-Nosed Buddha.

A Review of the Hong Kong and Macao Bloodlines

Most of our original Shar-Pei imports came from Taiwan, Hong Kong, and Macao (Portuguese China). Because the immediate ancestors of the Taiwanese dogs came themselves, for the greater part, from Hong Kong and Macao, it is in these two centers that an examination of the records provides us with a basis for the study of our bloodlines.

Macao has long been prominent in the history of the Shar-Pei for several reasons. Less than a hundred years ago, before British control of Hong Kong trade, Macao was a primary center for exports flowing from Southern China to the West. Naturally, ties with China were extremely close and the dogs of Southern China were popular in Macao. Eventually the trade importance of Macao declined to the point where, today, most of the revenues are derived from gambling and other illegal activities.

But in spite of this, the Shar-Pei has not been completely abandoned, as Mr. Strang discovered on a visit to Macao in the fall of 1977. Fairly good specimens may still be found in scattered homes throughout the area. And though most of these Macao Shar-Pei are nonpedigreed, both puppies and adults are eagerly sought out by fanciers from Hong Kong.

One reason that the dogs of Macao usually have no pedigree is the lack of interest there in organized kennel activities. But there is another reason also. Internal struggles in China over the last several decades have had the effect of driving illegal refugees into neighboring countries and some of the Shar-Pei in Macao have undoubtedly arrived illegally with their masters. In this manner a small but constant flow of new Shar-Pei blood from China has become available to breeders elsewhere.

Fortunately for American breeders, records and pedigrees are maintained with the utmost care and fidelity in Hong Kong by the Hong Kong and Kowloon Kennel Association. This association was founded in the late 1960's, taking over Shar-Pei registrations from the Hong Kong Kennel Club, which had previously recorded them. The Kennel Association gave its first Championship Show in 1972 and has held spring and fall shows ever since.

The Association's records provide us with the names of the dogs brought into Hong Kong from Macao and the names of their owners. From these records we can follow the pedigrees of all registered Shar-Pei bred in the Crown Colony. And we find that dogs now being imported from Hong Kong may have several generations of registered ancestors fully authenticated.

By studying the pictures of these registered ancestors of our dogs we find the key to the bloodlines being made available to us. The following photographs are of important dogs in the Down-Homes Kennel of Mr. Matgo Law. A careful study of these pictures allows us to appreciate the continuing influence of these dogs in our breeding programs today.

Down-Homes Anne Revival. Note deep-set triangular eyes.

Down-Homes Little Cube (bitch) at six weeks of age.

Down-Homes Sweet Pea, one of the foundation studs at Down-Homes Kennels (now deceased).

Above, Down-Homes Hoi-Chee of Eshaf, at five weeks. Whelped October 20, 1975. By Down-Homes Clown-Nosed Buddha ex Down-Homes Harmony.

Above, Down-Homes Harmony, whelped June 9, 1971. Red bitch by Ah-Choi of Ming ex Ah-Chee. Best of Breed and Group Second under judge Vincent Perry at Hong Kong Show, March 30, 1975.

Above, Down-Homes "Little" litter at six weeks. Whelped 1971—one dog and three bitches. By Down-Homes Sweet Pea ex Down-Homes Anne Revival.

Above, Down-Homes Man Sang, whelped April 16, 1976. By Down-Homes Bobby ex Down-Homes Harmony. Breeder, Matgo Law. Owner, E. Ted Linn, Asheville, North Carolina.

Below, Down-Homes Un Long, whelped 1974. By Ferricape ex Darkie. This Shar-Pei has very small ears—thumb-nail size.

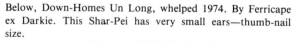

Below, Down-Homes Rust Copper—rare rust color, heavy bone. By Ah-Choi of Ming ex Sze-Yan-Mui of Ming.

Above, Down-Homes Mui-Chu, bitch, whelped in Macao and exported to Ernest W. Albright.

Above, Down-Homes Little Thunder at six weeks of age.

Another important source of bloodlines from Hong Kong is Yu Ying Wai's Chinese Diamond Kennels. Should this kennel prove able to proceed as planned, the dogs (as seen from the pictures below and on the following page) should prove to be a boon for Shar-Pei breeders everywhere.

Above, Down-Homes Oriental Pearl at five weeks. Exported from Hong Kong to Ellen Weathers.

Above, Down-Homes Black Pearl, litter mate of Oriental Pearl. Owner, Matgo Law.

Below, Ah Mei of Chinese Diamond at *four months* of age.

Below, Ah Fuk of Chinese Diamond.

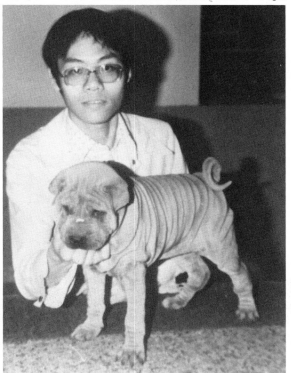

Above, Ah Ying of Chinese Diamond.

Above, full sister of Chinese Diamond Ah Fuk, pictured at two months of age.

Above, Chinese Diamond puppies at one and a half months of age. Owner, Yu Ying Wai, Hong Kong.

Above, Ah Choi of Chinese Diamond at eight months of age.

Below, Ah Fun of Chinese Diamond at two and a half years of age (1978).

Below, Ah Wah of Chinese Diamond, male, at eighteen months of age (1978).

Tips on Buying a Puppy

All prospective puppy purchasers should be aware that the AKC frowns on puppies of any breed being sold before they reach eight weeks of age. In buying a Shar-Pei puppy it is also appropriate to recall those wise words of Confucius, "Look before you leap."

The first step should be to familiarize yourself as much as possible with the puppy's genetic background. The best way to do this is to visit the kennel in order to examine the sire and dam.

If it is not possible to visit the kennel, ask for pictures of the parents and examine them carefully. Some breeders send out photos which may, or may not, be pictures of the actual parents. It is imperative to make sure on this point.

If pictures show dogs sitting down, their tails will not be visible. While the official Standards currently in use in the United States admit any sort of tail, the Chinese Standard requires a fairly short curled tail carried over the back. This type of tail certainly gives a Shar-Pei more allure than no tail at all or a short screw tail, or one of the straight tails of varying length sometimes seen.

Also beware of pictures showing the dogs lying down or standing in deep grass. Weak pasterns and splay feet, both very undesirable, may be hidden from view. Angulation should be good, and the topline should be straight.

The head is of vital importance. Make sure your prospective puppy's parents have the flat, strong, hippopotamus-type head with little stop, a broad blunt muzzle, the somewhat sunken and rather small triangular shaped dark eyes, and the typical, rather quizzical expression. The small ears, set on at the top of the skull, should not be upright or prick ears but should be folded, pointing towards the eyes.

Puppies are much more wrinkled than adults, but even so the adults should not look like Boxers. The face should be heavily wrinkled and there should be plenty of dewlap. There should be plenty of loose skin on the body, and most fanciers like to see a baggy-pants effect on the legs, especially around the hocks on the hindquarters.

Ask for copies of pedigrees and try to see pictures of as many of the ancestors as possible. Photos of a number of the important original imports appear in this book, and the breeder should have other photos available for your inspection. If your intended purchase is linebred on a dog with a pink nose, weak pasterns, or a short tail, you should remember that "blood will tell."

Size, weight, and general type of build vary to some extent. While the Shar-Pei is a medium-sized dog and the males usually are heavier and more strongly put together than the bitches, we do find some males with rather light bone and a somewhat willowy appearance. Since the Official Standards of both of the American Shar-Pei clubs call for a ". . . short coupled dog, well knit in frame, giving a square build, standing firm on the ground, with a calm and firm stature," these lightly constructed dogs leave something to be desired. Should you be choosing a male with, possibly, the intention of using him later at stud, you will naturally want a pup from a heavy-boned sire. Or, if you are picking a bitch for future breeding, again you will have bone and the "standing firm" admonition in mind.

Coats vary, too, but a short bristly coat is preferable. In the Orient this short coat is called the *horse** coat and another, longer type of coat, termed the *brush* coat is admitted. Undoubtedly, then, before arriving on these shores the two types have probably been interbred. This may well have been in an effort to preserve the breed at all cost when it faced extinction. In any case we do find the longer brush-coat puppies appearing from time to time in short-coat litters.

You must also remember that the spotted coat is a fault. Because "blood will tell," be sure that few of the ancestors carry this fault.

Once you have assembled all of the background information on the parents and grandparents and have studied the Shar-Pei Standards carefully, the bloodlines carried by the puppies, and the reputation of the breeder from whom you are buying, you probably will not be able to resist the urge

---

*At the 1979 National Specialty Show in California, Matgo Law explained to the members of the club that in China, horses have a short bristly coat, with the hair growing at an angle of 8°—rather than a smooth flat coat of the type that is typical of horses in the United States. And it is to a coat similar to that of the Chinese horse, Mr. Law said, that the Chinese refer when they speak of the Shar-Pei having a *horse* coat.

Above, Down-Homes Man Poon, by Down-Homes Bobby ex Down-Homes Harmony. Breeder, Matgo Law. Owner, Charles Murphy, Jr. Photographer, Ralph Martin.

Right, Down-Homes Man Poon at fifteen weeks.

Left, Wang So, by Chico's Roro II ex Ho Wun II Ling Ling. Breeder, Darlene A. Wright. Owner, Thomas V. Blanton, Jr., Richmond, Virginia.

Below, Scarsdale Chewbacca, whelped October 10, 1977, by Scarsdale's Chairman Mao ex Down-Homes Man Hing. Breeder, Patti Schwieterman. Owner, Ruth Fink, Elizabethtown, Pennsylvania.

to select your own little bundle of wiggles and wrinkles. Before making your final decision, you are almost sure to find yourself, flushed with pleasure, anxiety, and delight, right in the middle of a litter of plump, pudgy, roly-poly Shar-Pei puppies.

Be calm. Find a chair and sit down, if possible. All of the puppies, at first glance, will appear to be equally lovable. But take your time and go over each one in detail. Common sense, and a firm grip on your emotions, will prevent any serious mistake.

Watch carefully as the puppies tussle and play. Pay special attention to those that are the most active, alert, and full of vitality. Those that shrink away when spoken to, or that attempt to run away and hide, can be classified as shy. They may overcome this characteristic later, but taking the chance is not worthwhile.

If the breeder has given the proper vaccines, he will not mind if you pick up the puppies one at a time. Examine them first head-on. Look for a broad, blunt muzzle, small eyes, plenty of wrinkles, and small ears. The pigment should be strong; the nose black and shining; the tongue, lips, and eyerims the same. Staining below the inner corner of the eye indicates weeping. This may be only a passing phase, but it can indicate such future troubles as blocked tear glands, loose lids, an allergy, or inverted eyelashes.

Raise the lips and check the gums. They should be healthy-looking. The gums of puppies that need worming have a pallid look and, often, such puppies have bad breath.

Look at the teeth. The upper and lower front teeth may meet edge to edge (an even bite), or overlap slightly as do the blades of a scissors. A gap between the upper and lower teeth indicates that the bite is either undershot or overshot.

Check inside the ears. They should be clean, sweet-smelling, and free of accumulated dirt or wax. The position of the ears—set wide apart and well forward over the eyes—can usually be appreciated at this age.

Next check the condition of the puppy's skin. It should be clean and free of rash, eczema, and fleas. And it should be loose and heavily wrinkled—so much so that you can gather it up by the handful without disturbing the pup.

As the pups move about and play, watch especially for those that seem to dominate their mates. In a tussling match the stronger pup keeps his balance, while the weaker pup rolls over and gives up. The stronger pup usually has a better rear—the hindquarters set well apart, with good angulation—and very often strength in the rear gives a pup more backbone.

Thus a blocky pup, one that is built like a tank, is usually a better prospect than a lanky one. Pay attention, too, to the front legs. They should be straight, with good bone. Splay feet and weak pasterns can already be noted at a very early age.

Check the tail. It should be set on high, clearly exposing the anus. Make sure the dewclaws have been removed from the rear feet. The back should be broad and strong.

When examining the male puppies, palpate them to see that both testicles are descended. A dog without two fully descended testicles is automatically disqualified in the show ring under American Kennel Club rules. Further, a dog without two fully descended testicles should not be used for breeding because this is an inherited fault.

After you have finished a careful physical examination of all the pups and have watched them as they move about, take a bit of extra time and look for the psychological properties of stance, bearing, charisma, and *gestalt*. Almost all puppies are cute, and many fulfill the physical properties we desire, but in most litters there will be some that have a certain something extra. In the Shar-Pei we want a lordly stance and scowl. A monarch who looks down on all he surveys—but who loves his master.

Once you have made your decision, do not forget in the euphoria of the moment that there are still quite a few details to iron out before you write your check. Your Shar-Pei puppies are rather expensive and it is good to have the as-

surance that you will receive advice and counsel on the pup from the breeder in future weeks. And be sure to ask for the pup's registration papers and pedigree, and information as to when his puppy shots were given and exactly what they were. The so-called measles vaccine is usually given at three weeks and a combination distemper, hepatitis, leptospirosis, and para-influenza (DHLP) shot at seven weeks of age. A second DHLP shot is usually given at ten weeks.

Also ask the breeder to provide you with a health certificate from a veterinarian, and with the puppy's diet sheet. You may want to change the diet later on, but when moving a young animal into new surroundings it is important that his food, at least, be recognizable to him.

When the puppy arrives at his new home you should, as soon as possible, make an appointment with your own veterinarian and have him examine the dog. The excitement of the trip could have caused a stress problem, so by having your veterinarian check the puppy immediately, you can avoid any incipient trouble almost before it starts. Also have your veterinarian check again for worms even though the puppy is supposedly worm-free.

Take along and show your veterinarian the diet sheet and health certificate given you by the breeder. As long as your veterinarian is going to have your prize possession under his care, he may want to make suggestions regarding care, feeding, and diet supplements.

After the pup has had a few days rest and has begun to feel at home in his new surroundings, you can, at last, call your friends and alert the local newspaper. The urge to share the joy of actually owning one of these heart-stealing Chinese bandits will be overwhelming.

Down-Homes Ningpo of Starlaxy, by Down-Homes China Faith ex Down-Homes Lady Charcoal. Breeder, Matgo Law. Owner, Dr. Robert M. Brown, Jackson, Wisconsin.

Albright's Ho Wun Me Kong, by Chico's Roro II ex Albright's Hang Mao. Breeder, Ernest Albright. Owner, Thomas Fritts.

Above, Chen Chu, bitch owned by Mr. and Mrs. Walter "Dugan" Skinner, Wolcottville, Indiana. Her puppy picture is in the 1978 *Guinness Book of World Records.*

Above, Ping (Siskiyou's Pekka-Ling), by J. C. Smith's Gwei-Loh ex Down-Homes Little Pea. Breeder, Lois Alexander. Owner, Nancy Dumay, Missoula, Montana.

Above, Shir Du Ling Fu and Cup Cake, owned by Mr. and Mrs. Walter "Dugan" Skinner, Wolcottville, Indiana.

Below, Shir Du Ling Fu at eight months of age.

Above, Shir Du Ling Fu at three months of age.

Below, Shir Du Ling Fu at two years of age.

FEEDING

In the Orient dogs are generally not so well cared for as they are in this country. They seldom receive veterinary attention and are fed mostly on rice or sustain themselves by scavenging. As a result, some dogs develop rickets, splay feet, or weak pasterns. A dog imported quite early and provided proper nutrition and medical care will not usually be subject to these problems.

In Hong Kong the Shar-Pei is often fed on freshly cooked rice mixed with shredded fish. The fish supplies protein and the rice completes the diet by supplying carbohydrates, fiber, and bulk.

American veterinarians no longer recommend a steady diet of fish, either for dogs or cats. The feeling is that a prolonged use of fish as the main source of protein can lead to nutritional deficiencies.

Fortunately, the Shar-Pei has switched happily from the Chinese-style cuisine to our American fare and seems to prosper on any of our handy American dog foods.

Many fanciers use the dry food which may be either kibbled biscuit or meal, or the chow-style formed nuggets. Dry food is usually mixed with water, milk, broth, or meat, according to the directions on the package. Some breeders add extra fat such as corn oil. Others may mix in cottage cheese or scrambled eggs. It is important to not add too much in the form of tidbits, or the dog will pick these out and leave the balanced ration in his dish.

Canned dog food is fed by some. This has less than half the amount of protein found in the dry food and, being super-soft, does not afford the dog chewing pleasure. But it can be added to the dry food as a flavor enhancer.

A third type of dog food is the soft-moist diet that comes disguised as hamburger and contains sugar, salt, and a good deal of coloring dyes. The dogs like it and it, too, can be used in conjunction with the dry food, or as an alternative if the dog tires of his regular ration.

Shar-Pei puppies should be fed small amounts three times a day up to five months of age and twice a day to ten months of age. Adults should be fed larger amounts once a day. There are special dry foods formulated expressly for puppies and these give excellent results. During the puppy stage many people like to moisten the food with milk. If this is done, a raw egg yolk to one cup of milk further fortifies the meal. If moistened food is used, be sure to let it stand for half an hour to allow the food to expand.

Food should be left down only until the dogs walk away, when the dish should be removed. Especially in warm weather, there can be a bacteria build-up in the food which could cause illness in puppies, and in older Shar-Pei as well.

Shar-Pei often need their jowls wiped after eating, for if food is permitted to dry on the skin, a rash sometimes develops. Wiping the jowls clean with a dampened cloth will eliminate the possibility that irritation will develop.

In feeding both puppies and adults it is important to remember that over-feeding leads to trouble. An overfed dog does not exercise properly, and activity is essential for normal growth and condition.

Fresh clean water should be available to a dog at all times. Stainless steel pans and bowls are best both for feeding and watering. The plastic dishes so often used are frequently chewed up by both puppies and adult dogs, and plastic bits and pieces are not good things for any dog to swallow. Stainless steel dishes are expensive to start with but cheaper in the long run, for they don't wear out. They are easy to clean and don't tip over easily if the proper sizes and shapes are selected.

Ta-Ho, owned by Gary Raser, Royal City, Washington.

HOUSEBREAKING

Shar-Pei puppies are naturally clean and usually easy to housebreak. Newspapers are used, and by placing the puppy on paper when he has to go, he soon gets the idea. Walking the dog a few minutes after he has eaten is the second step. Most puppies turn away from the food dish when they are full, and relieve themselves almost immediately. With older dogs there is a greater lapse of time. By taking the dog (either puppy or adult) outdoors after he has finished eating, and immediately after he awakens in the morning or from a nap, he becomes accustomed to outdoor relief. All dogs are creatures of habit, and they soon learn to understand the reprimand should they forget themselves indoors.

GROOMING AND BATHING

The cardinal rule in bathing a dog is to never do it at all if you are in a hurry. Take your time. Use lukewarm water and mild soap or shampoo. Soap residue left on the Shar-Pei's skin will cause dryness and itching, so rinse thoroughly and then rinse again. Because the coat is subject to dryness and the skin easily irritated, baby oil or Alpha Keri may be used in the last rinse. Do not let the dog outdoors while he is wet. A wet or damp dog that gets chilled outdoors or by lying close to an air-conditioner can come down with pneumonia. Be sure to use plenty of towels and be sure the dog is completely dry as quickly as possible.

Actually, the Shar-Pei can usually be kept clean either by giving him a rubdown with a damp towel or by brushing. The best brushes are those with medium-hard natural bristles. Wire, or even nylon bristles, can irritate the skin.

Keep the toenails trimmed. This is especially important with young puppies, for in roughhousing together, there is the danger of one puppy's nail puncturing the eye of another. A special nail clipper for dogs makes the job easy. By holding the nail to the light, the interior blood vessel can usually be seen and by cutting beyond its extremity there will be no bleeding. If the nail should bleed, a bit of vaseline held to the cut will stop the bleeding in a short time. Nervous owners often have this job done by a veterinarian.

Pay special attention to the insides of the ears. A tiny mite often sets up housekeeping in a dog's ears, causing the dog to shake his head frequently, scratch his ears, and whine. Wax builds up deep in the ear canal. In attempting to clean out the ear, there is always a danger of pushing the wax plug deeper down. The best solution for this possible problem is to keep a sharp watch on the ears and certainly have them checked at every trip the dog makes to the veterinarian. Here, also, the veterinarian can provide proper medication and instructions for treatment.

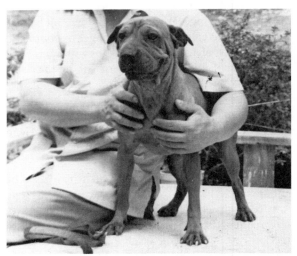

Young bitch at Hong Kong kennels of Robert Chan, 1977.

Chinese Shar-Pei at Ohio Rare Breed Club Show, 1977.

WORMING

All puppies and all adult dogs are likely to harbor internal parasites. In puppies a bloated stomach is often a sign of round worms. A staring coat, lack of appetite, general lassitude, vomiting, and diarrhea are other signs that the dog may need worming. Your veterinarian can do a stool check with a microscope and, by identifying the worm eggs and determining which kind infest the animal, can recommend the proper treatment. The fact that the microscope reveals no worm eggs does not always mean the dog is not infested. Rather, it may mean that the parasites were not propagating at that time. A second stool examination the following day would provide a safe check.

TATTOOING

Dogs get lost and dogs get stolen, but if an animal carries an identifying tattoo number on the inside of an ear or the inside of a rear leg, there is a ninety percent chance that he will eventually be recovered. Tattooing can be done by your veterinarian for a small fee, and there are a number of registries that will record the number and help you locate the dog in the event he disappears.

The buzz of the needle may cause apprehension on the part of the dog, but it is virtually painless. Either your own Social Security Number or the dog's registration number can be used. In the case of the Shar-Pei, having this done is an absolute must. Many people will covet your dog but will think twice if he is tattooed.

Fritts' Hai Chopper Ho, whelped December 31, 1977. Breeder, James Weathers. Owner, Joyce Fritts, Erie, Pennsylvania.

Chinese Shar-Pei at Matgo Law's kennel in Hong Kong.

HOUSING

While the Shar-Pei is widely known as an all-purpose dog, he could equally well be known as an all-weather dog. Fanciers have discovered that this is a breed that adapts to any climate. The dogs are doing well in the hot, humid South, in Northern latitudes, on the East Coast, in the Midwest, in the deserts of the West, as well as in the Northern and Southern California areas.

Because of his relatively moderate size, the Shar-Pei does extremely well as a house dog. He loves to romp and play, so muscle-toning can be provided by teaching him to retrieve a rubber ball.

The Shar-Pei is a very sturdy breed and, if desired, he can be kept in confined quarters out-of-doors for short periods of the day. A nice clean dog house and a modest-sized fenced-in area (safe from automobiles) will keep him happy. Shade should be provided and many owners like to give the dog a raised bench on which he can sit or lie down when he is outdoors.

It is important to remember that dogs (especially young dogs) must have human companionship throughout much of the day in order to develop a well-rounded personality. Scientific studies show that the most critical period in personality development is between six and ten weeks of age, so it is during this period particularly that the owner must plan to spend a good deal of time each day with his dog.

31

Above, Tomb Dog—courtesy of Mr. Bowman Stevens.

Above, Tomb Dogs—courtesy of Mr. Bowman Stevens.

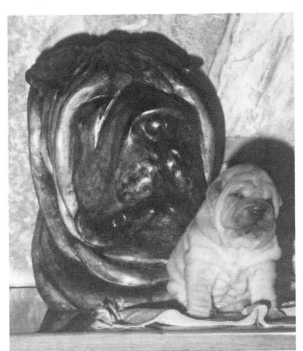

Above, Shir Du Doll Lee at eighteen days of age. Out of Cup Cake and Foo Foo. Breeder, Walter "Dugan" Skinner.

Above, Han Statuette, 500 B.C., Fine Arts Museum, Florence, Italy.

Below, Chinese Han statuette, 300 B.C., Chernushi Museum, Italy.

Below, Paul Strang's Han statuette, 500 B.C.

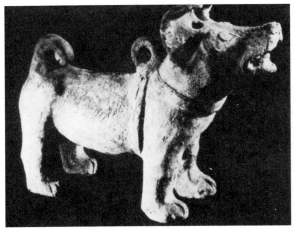

Breeding and Whelping

The Shar-Pei bitch comes in season twice a year (some more often), usually starting at nine months of age. Breeding your bitch the first time at eighteen months of age and thereafter only once a year is the only proper way to keep a healthy and humane outlook.

But long before breeding time you will probably have spent "umpteen" hours going over your bitch's pedigree and trying to match it for best results with pedigrees of a number of stud dogs.

If the bitch has a short tail, lack of sufficient wrinkling, or entropion, you will not want a dog with these same defects. In fact, the axiom in breeding is, "never breed a fault to the same fault."

In selecting a stud it is also wise to choose one that has previously sired a litter. And by all means make an effort to see his get and evaluate the type of offspring he is siring. If you are considering the possible use of a dog that has never sired a litter, it is a good policy to ask the owner to have a sperm count done on the dog by his veterinarian. This is easy to do and gives you the assurance as to whether or not the stud is capable of siring puppies. With a weak sperm count, chances are slim.

When you have finally chosen the stud you wish to use, make a reservation for his service. The terms should be specific and in writing. Never risk waiting until the bitch is already in season to settle terms with the stud's owner.

The price for stud service varies. Some owners want all cash. Some will take one or two pups in return for the service. And others will take part cash plus first, second, or third choice from the litter. Whatever the agreement, it is imperative to put it all down in writing, for this will forestall any future disagreements.

The following is not intended as a complete and comprehensive discourse on breeding and whelping but is simply a brief explanation of what is to be expected when a Shar-Pei bitch enters her heat cycle, is bred at the proper time, and whelps a litter of puppies. Any Shar-Pei owner who is interested in breeding should study several of the books on canine genetics and breeding and whelping that are currently available. Two excellent works covering these subjects are *Meisen Breeding Manual,* by Hilda Meisenzahl, and *The Standard Book of Dog Breeding,* by Dr. Alvin Grossman—both published by the publisher of this book.

Red staining from the vagina signifies the beginning of the heat cycle, and from the tenth to the sixteenth day is considered the most propitious time for breeding. Swelling of the vagina will be apparent before this occurs. When the bitch is ready, she will stand for the dog and cooperate to some degree with his efforts. Some breeders believe it worthwhile to assist with the breeding and "help" the male. With some breeds that are neurotic and over-bred this may be necessary, but Shar-Pei are normal animals and able, usually, to work things out on their own.

It goes without saying that the bitch as well as the male should be in tiptop condition. Make sure that your bitch is current on all her shots, and many fanciers think it advisable for a bitch to have had a DHLP booster shot before breeding. Also, the bitch should be free of worms. Another precaution is to have an examination made both before and after the breeding to be sure there is no sign of a vaginal infection.

When the bitch and the dog are brought together, the dog usually "courts" the bitch until she is ready to accept him and to allow him to mount her, whereupon he will go over her back and she will turn her tail sideways, allowing him to penetrate the vagina. When the penis enters the vagina, it swells and enlarges until it is several times its normal size, while the muscles of the vagina grasp it spasmodically. This facilitates prolonged copulation, which is known as a "tie." Once the two are tied, the male will turn around so he and the female are standing back-to-back.

In a successful mating the dogs will usually remain tied back-to-back for fifteen or twenty minutes. Some breeders like to have a repeat breeding a day later, if possible, just to make sure the bitch is really bred.

While the normal gestation period in dogs is sixty-three days, some breeders report many Shar-Pei litters are whelped sooner—sometimes as early as the fifty-eighth day.

The whelping quarters should be prepared at least a week in advance. Most breeders use a wooden whelping box five feet square with sides

Above, Albright's Lou Mang with litter of puppies. Lou Mang, bred by Ernest Albright, is by Albright's Ling Hsiu ex Smith's Ho Ho. Owner, Ruth Fink, Elizabethtown, Pennsylvania.

Above, puppies bred by Robert W. Cook, East Berlin, Pennsylvania.

Below, part of a litter of December 1974 from Down-Homes Little Pea. Breeder-owner, Lois E. Alexander, San Luis Obispo, California.

six to eight inches high, and line the bottom of the box with clean, flat newspapers. Before the whelping date, the bitch will gradually become used to the box and, as her time draws near, will do a lot of digging and pawing to make a "nest." This rumples up the papers, so they must be changed. Otherwise, when the puppies do arrive, they could become lost in the rubble.

Because of the possibility that you may need help, it is always a good idea to alert your veterinarian when whelping seems imminent. Then if his services are required, you will be able to get in touch with him immediately.

Several hours before actual whelping begins, muscular contractions manifest themselves in the form of ripples running down the sides of the mother-to-be. A sudden gush of greenish fluid from the vaginal canal indicates that the water or fluid surrounding the puppies has "broken" and that the puppies are about to start to emerge. Puppies are whelped about half an hour apart, though a longer or shorter time may occur between births. Never should more than two hours elapse, however. If the bitch has abdominal contractions for two hours without producing a puppy, you must seek veterinary assistance at once.

As each puppy emerges, the bitch will lick it rapidly, cut the navel cord, remove the sac in which the puppy is encased, and then swallow the afterbirth, which contains nutritional qualities that give her the stimulation she needs during her ordeal. A new mother may cut the cord and not remove the sac immediately, or she may not take care of her newborn at all. Your assistance is needed here. The sac is a transparent membrane in which the puppy is encased at birth, and if it is not removed from the puppy's face immediately, the puppy will be unable to breathe and will die.

Keeping the family warm and out of drafts is most important at this time. Most breeders remove the puppies as they are whelped, dry them thoroughly, and keep them warm in a basket away from the mother where she cannot hear their little whines and yelps. Before placing a puppy in the basket, Tincture of Merthiolate or Iodine may be applied to the end of the navel cord.

When the bitch has finished whelping, which with the Shar-Pei means anywhere from four to eight little ones, the puppies are returned to the dam. Each will find a nipple and start to nurse. If any seem hesitant or weak they should be helped by placing them up to a nipple, opening their mouths with gentle pressure on both sides of the jaws, and inserting the nipple into the mouth.

Some Shar-Pei are whelped with dewclaws. A dewclaw is a fifth toe high on the leg and without purpose to the foot. Dewclaws on the front legs are acceptable, but if dewclaws are present on the hind legs they should be removed about the third day by your veterinarian.

It is wise to have a veterinarian examine both dam and pups within twenty-four hours after the last pup is whelped. And, of course, during whelping if all does not seem to be going well, call your veterinarian for advice. If he can't come to you, arrange to meet him at his office. Bundle dam and pups into the car and get there as quickly as possible. Don't panic. Just be sure to get help if you think you need it. If this is your first litter, it would probably be a good idea also to have the help, or at least the phone number, of an experienced breeder on whom you can call for assistance.

Puppies open their eyes by degrees. At ten days you can usually see a little slit beginning between upper and lower lids. The slit gradually widens and at twelve or fourteen days the eyes are fully open, although the faculty of sight is not yet fully developed. The biggest problem in the breed is entropian, the turning in of the eyelids. You should watch for it, and if you note any apparent abnormality of the eyelids, you should seek veterinary assistance at once.

At about three weeks of age extra nourishment should be offered, though the puppies may not want it. Most breeders use one of the puppy chows mixed with milk and mushed to pap in an electric blender. It should then be offered in a low pan or pans. Although some of the puppies may start to eat at this age, especially if the dam's milk is beginning to taper off, most will walk in it, sit in it, or go to sleep in the pan—and they will get covered with the food. Use a damp cloth to keep the puppies clean, and keep trying. Within a week or so all will usually have gotten the idea that what you are offering is food for them to eat, and from then on the problem is over and weaning well on its way.

As soon as the puppies are eating on their own —usually at three and a half weeks—take stool samples to the veterinarian for a worm check. Most puppies have worms, so all are usually wormed at three to four weeks of age. Continue to have the stools checked at regular intervals for the next several months, at least. When you take in the first stool samples, ask about shots. Some vets like to give a so-called "measles shot" at three weeks. This is a modified distemper and hepatitis vaccine. Then follow your veterinarian's advice as to the rest of the shots your dog will need. Giving the dogs a good start in life ensures strong, happy, healthy dogs later on. And remember—one of yours may someday have a chance at being the biggest show winner of all time.

When first whelped, Shar-Pei puppies may not be any more wrinkled than puppies of other breeds. But by the time they are five weeks old, head and body will be enveloped in the typical accordion-like pleats. In the following months they will gradually become less wrinkled as they grow into their skin. But then, as young adults, the pleats reappear and the appearance of the dog tends to revert to the way he looked as a puppy. Naturally, the extent of the wrinkles in a puppy or an adult is governed by the animal's bloodline.

With any new litter of Shar-Pei puppies the parade of friends and fellow-fanciers will begin. Be prepared. Some of your visitors will undoubtedly be "experts" who will be only too happy to point out to you all of the puppies' faults. Some of these experts may not stop at what is wrong with the pups but will also enumerate the faults of the sire and dam as well. Much of this fault-finding should be viewed as constructive criticism emphasizing the need to refrain from producing poor specimens during this critical period when the breed is being rebuilt.

And, of course, there is a great deal of truth in such admonitions. But there is another side of the coin that must be considered, too. We are dealing with an endangered species for which there is, at present, no official AKC Standard. Indiscriminate culling at the present time could risk removing valuable assets from our scanty genetic pool. It is possible that a puppy displaying what one person considers a serious fault could, conceivably, be perfectly acceptable, even valuable, for future breeding. Your best bet, then, is not to be discouraged if some of your puppies display one fault or another. You may decide to try a different combination of bloodlines for future breeding. And in the meantime, let the pups grow up a little before deciding, definitely, which males should be neutered and which females should be spayed.

Above, Ha Chew, owned by Jack and Bettye Small,

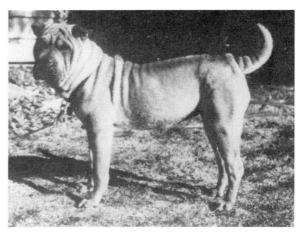

Above, Tara, at one year of age. Owner, Ernest Albright. Tara was featured in the movie *The Billion Dollar Hobo* with Tim Conway.

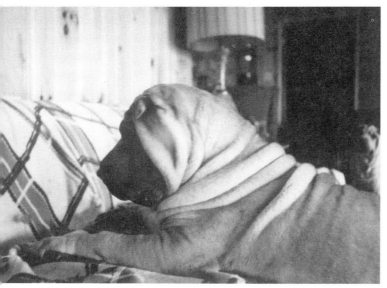

Above, Down-Homes Gem, bred by Matgo Law.

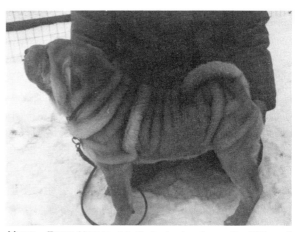

Above, Down-Homes Ah-Q (note brush coat). This red male, by Down-Homes Jim Jade ex Down-Homes Don Kar, was whelped in Hong Kong on September 12, 1977. Breeder, Matgo Law. Owner, Annabelle Linn, Asheville, North Carolina.

Below, Guei-Loh, male, at four months of age. Owner, Ernest W. Albright.

Opal, bred and owned by Annabelle and E. Ted Linn, Asheville, North Carolina.

Showing Your Shar-Pei

The first thing you will discover in showing your Shar-Pei is that no matter where you go, this breed is bound to attract more attention than all the rest of the dogs put together.

Since The American Kennel Club requires that there must first be at least 650 specimens of a breed and at least five generations of true breeding carried out by fanciers located in different areas of the country, the Shar-Pei is not yet (1979) eligible for competition in licensed AKC shows. But in the meantime, the Shar-Pei can be shown at local matches and take part in the rare breed shows that are given in various areas.

The show held annually by the New England club known as Associated Rare Breeds—New England, sets the standard for all shows of this type held throughout the United States. Entries are open to all purebred rare breeds which are not presently eligible for registration with The American Kennel Club.

However, a breed must have a Standard and be registered with a recognized national or international kennel club. And, any breed not presently listed as eligible for competition may apply to the show committee, which will review the application.

Besides the Shar-Pei, breeds presently accepted by the Associated Rare Breeds—New England Club include: Canaan Dog, Small Muensterlander, Spinoni Italiani, Ibizan Hound, American Eskimo Dog, Australian Cattle Dog, Australian Kelpie, Australian Shepherd Dog, Border Collie, Catahoula Leopard Dog, American Pit Bull Terrier, Miniature Bull Terrier, Cavalier King Charles Spaniel, Chinese Crested Dog, Little Lion Dog, Finnish Spitz, Amertoy, Xoloitzcuintli, Greater Swiss Mountain Dog, Tibetan Spaniel, and Neapolitan Mastiff.

The Associated Rare Breeds—New England Club, Inc., was started in 1971 by Mrs. Jay Child, who wanted a place or a show at which to exhibit her Tibetan Spaniels. The goal, as she saw it then and which has been overwhelmingly success-ful, was twofold: 1. A show run along the lines of an American Kennel Club Plan-A Match to acquaint novice owners of rare breeds wishing registration with the AKC as to exactly how an AKC show is run. 2. To acquaint AKC licensed judges with these rare breeds.

The catalog of this show goes world-wide, and a copy of each year's catalog is retained as a permanent record by the AKC, whose delegates and board members also attend the show. All Shar-Pei owners should certainly make every effort to attend rare breed shows. For further information on rare breed shows, write: The American Kennel Club, Inc., 51 Madison Avenue, New York, NY 10010, and ask for the name and address of the current Secretary of the Shar-Pei Club of America, Inc., who will be glad to provide information on shows and show dates.

Rare breed shows are held in New York, New Jersey, Ohio, Michigan, and Canada, and on the West Coast. In order to learn about the exact places and dates of the different shows, fanciers could also contact their local dog show organization and keep in touch with other Shar-Pei owners, as well.

In preparing the Shar-Pei for a show, the dog should be well-socialized and perfectly accustomed to crowds of people and dogs. He should be leash-trained, of course, so that he "struts his stuff" with vigor and enthusiasm. He should be clean and well-groomed. Most fanciers do not cut the Shar-Pei's whiskers, feeling that they add to his haughty Chinese look.

Since the judge will want to open the mouth to examine the teeth and the tongue, the dog should be accustomed to this sort of invasion of his privacy by strangers. Also, if the Shar-Pei is a male, he should allow the judge to determine whether he has both testicles descended.

One last thought: Newspaper photographers usually cover the rare breed shows, and since the Shar-Pei gets the lion's share of the attention, the owner, too, should be well turned out.

Above, Tara (bitch) at four months of age. Owner, Ernest W. Albright.

Above, Shir Du Pu Ko Ti at twelve weeks of age. Owners, Mr. and Mrs. Walter "Dugan" Skinner.

Above, Shir Du Yen Se at three months of age. Bred and owned by Mr. and Mrs. Walter "Dugan" Skinner.

Above, puppy from the kennels of Matgo Law.

Above, Siskiyou's Pekka Ling, bred by Lois Alexander and owned by Nancy Dumav.

Above, puppy from Matgo Law's Down-Home Kennels.

Above, five-week-old puppies from the Shir Du Kennels of Mr. and Mrs. Walter "Dugan" Skinner.

Left, Ro-Geans Ling Ming, owned by Raymond Anderson.

Right, Walnut Lane's Shao-Nu, owned by Raymond Anderson.

The Chinese Shar-Pei Clubs of America

Because of the ever-increasing popularity of the breed here in America, we now have three clubs devoted to furthering the interests of the breed. They are:

1. The Original Chinese Shar-Pei Club of America, Inc., P.O. Box 6512, Concord, California 94524. Organized 1974. Officers are: President, Ernest Albright, 24 Audrey Lane, Pleasant Hill, California, 94523; Vice-President, Walter (Dugan) Skinner, Box 388, Wolcottville, Indiana 46795; Secretary-Treasurere, Darlene Wright, 3207 Sheffield Place, Concord, California 94512; and Editor of the Newsletter, Susan Tunzi, 4497 Old Adobe Road, Petaluma, California 94952.

2. The Chinese Shar-Pei Club of America, Inc., Route 6, Box 398, Asheville, North Carolina 28730. Organized 1978. Officers are: President, E. Ted Linn, Route 6, Box 398, Asheville, North Carolina 28730; Vice-President, Victor Seas, 182 Whetstone River Road South, Route 2, Caledonia, Ohio 43314; Corresponding Secretary, Pat Pagnard, Route 1, County Road 72, Morral, Ohio 43337; Treasurer, Wilma Smith, 435½ North Fourth Street, Upper Sandusky, Ohio 43351; and Registrar, De Jon (Dee) Seas, Route 2, Box 89, Caledonia, Ohio 43314.

3. The Southern California Chinese Shar-Pei Club. Organized 1979 and an affiliate of The Original Chinese Shar-Pei Club of America. Officers are: President, Jim Weathers, 27341 Ortega Highway, San Juan Capistrano, California 92675; Vice-President, Roy Parker, P.O. Box 59383, Los Angeles, California 90061; Recording Secretary and Treasurer, Jack Small, 1425 East Belmont, Ontario, California 91761; Corresponding Secretary, Linda Gaetan, 5166 Glen View Place, Bonia, California 92002; and Show Chairman, Ellen Weathers, 27341 Ortega Highway, San Juan Capistrano, California 92675.

The first of these clubs, The Original Chinese Shar-Pei Club of America, came into being as a result of the first organizational meeting of American owners of Chinese Shar-Pei. This meeting was held on April 26, 1974, at the home of Mr. and Mrs. Carl Sanders, Ashland, Oregon. Those present besides Mr. and Mrs. Sanders included Mr. and Mrs. John Purcell of Ashland, Oregon; Mr.

Founding members of The Original Chinese Shar-Pei Club of America, Inc. Center, Lois E. Alexander. Right, Ernest Albright. Left, Mr. and Mrs. John Purcell. Center right, Mr. and Mrs. Carl Sanders.

Ernest W. Albright of Pleasant Hill, California; and Mrs. Lois Alexander of Talent, Oregon. Mr. Tom Parker of Vida, Oregon, was unable to attend because of illness, but two of his Shar-Pei were there for the others to admire.

It was at this meeting that after a tally of questionnaires was completed, the name of the breed was decided upon—Chinese Shar-Pei. It was also voted to name the organization The Chinese Shar-Pei Club of America.

Carl Sanders was appointed Acting President; Lois Alexander was appointed Acting Membership Secretary (to maintain a membership file and record of dogs owned, for AKC purposes); John Purcell was made Acting Treasurer; and Ernest Albright was asked to be responsible for research work on a Shar-Pei Standard; and Mrs. Dee Seas was delegated to set up and maintain the Stud Book for individual registration of all known purebred Shar-Pei, the members agreeing that this work should begin as soon as possible.

At that time—April 26, 1974—there were thirteen known owners of Shar-Pei in the United States, having a total of twenty-seven dogs. Owners and dogs were as follows:

OWNER	DOG'S NAME	SEX	AGE OR DATE OF WHELPING	PLACE OF OF WHELPING
Ernest W. Albright 24 Audrey Lane Pleasant Hill, CA	Mui-Chu China Souel (Chin)	Bitch Dog	June 1971 Oct. 21, 1973	Macao Hong Kong
Lois E. Alexander 2922 Anderson Creek Rd. Talent, OR	Down-Homes Little Pea Wohng Tohng Cho-Chi	Bitch Bitch Bitch	Nov. 17, 1971 Nov. 28, 1973 Nov. 28, 1971	Macao Oregon Oregon
Otto Dubell Star Route Vida, OR	Su Lin	Bitch	1 year	Oregon
Jean Fein 378 E. Loveland Loveland, OH	Down-Homes China Hope	Bitch	Oct. 21, 1973	Hong Kong
Lenee Kriseloff 8 Edgewood Court Persippany, NJ	Kung Hei	Bitch	May 1973	Macao
Renee Lew 1457 Hiawatha Ave. Hillside, NJ	Tit Lil (Iron Tongue)	Dog	Aug. 5, 1973	Hong Kong David Lee, breeder
Tom Parker Star Route Vida, OR	Ying Yang	Dog Bitch	2 years 2 years	Arizona Arizona
John Purcell 920 Wilson Road Ashland, OR	Bok Si Young (White Velvet)	Bitch	Nov. 28, 1973	Oregon
Carl Sanders Star Route Vida, OR	Yu-Lin Su-Su Ti-Ping Guy Fong Guy Lung	Bitch Bitch Bitch Dog Dog	3½ years 3½ years 4 months 2½ years 1 year	California Arizona Oregon Arizona Oregon
Darwin B. Smith 2527 E. Indianapolis Fresno, CA		Dog Bitch Bitch (spayed)		
J. C. Smith 5759 W. Indianola Phoenix, AZ	Chow Chow Bigoo Roro "Dumb Dumb"	Bitch Dog Bitch Bitch	6 years	Hong Kong Hong Kong Hong Kong Hong Kong
Mrs. Victor (Dee) Seas Walnut Lane Kennel 182 Whetstone River Rd. So. Caledonia, OH	Kung Fu China Love	Dog Bitch	May 23, 1973 Oct. 1973	Macao Hong Kong
Sue Weaver Weathree Kennels Route 1 Plymouth, IN			Mar. 3, 1974	Hong Kong

Above and below, Ho Wun II Chooey Sahm Phideau and Ho Wun II Ping Pong, owned by Pat Crawford, Albuquerque, New Mexico.

Below, Robert Chan of Hong Kong with his two-year-old male (1977).

Noting that differences in type were apparent among these dogs—particularly as to tail length and carriage, breadth of muzzle and abundance of wrinkles—the Club, at this first meeting, voted to strive for uniformity in the breed.

The second organizational meeting of the Club was held on July 27, 1974, at the home of Lois Alexander, Talent, Oregon. Present, when the meeting was called to order by Acting Secretary Lois Alexander because of the absence of Acting President Carl Sanders, were Ernest and Madeline Albright and John and Nadine Purcell. Carl Sanders and Renee Lew telephoned comments. Renee Lew was appointed official representative to the AKC and was requested to present an annual report to the AKC beginning in April 1975. Member Sue Weaver was asked to prepare and illustrate a brochure on the breed, to be used to answer questions on the breed that were pouring in from all parts of the country.

The third organizational meeting was held on November 3, 1974, at the home of Ernest and Madeline Albright, Pleasant Hill, California. The members present voted to join the National Rare Breed Club, and set up a point system for a Shar-Pei Specialty Match. They also discussed the Group in which the Shar-Pei should be shown and decided upon Non-Sporting.

The fourth organizational meeting was held on February 22, 1976, at the home of Ernest and Madeline Albright, Pleasant Hill, California. At this time there were nine members of the Club. (By April 25, 1976, there were nineteen members.) Those present besides Ernest and Madeline Albright, were Darlene Wright, also of Pleasant Hill, California; Mr. and Mrs. Walter DeLear of Los Altos, California; Anum Kealemakia of Daly City, California; John and Nadine Purcell of Ashland, Oregon; Lois Alexander of Talent, Oregon; and Walter (Dugan) and Shirley Skinner of Wolcottville, Indiana. All were Shar-Pei owners. Also present at the meeting was Jayne Langdon, dog show photographer, of Alameda, California.

It was at this meeting that the members voted on and passed the thirty-two statement *Official Standard of the Chinese Shar-Pei Club of America*—to be effective until 1981, when it will have been used for five years in accordance with AKC regulations. At this meeting the name of the breed was again voted on and confirmed as the Chinese Shar-Pei.

Also, at this fourth organizational meeting members learned the results of a survey on Shar-Pei in

Above, Willowledge puppies owned by Eve C. Olsen.

Above and below, Willowledge Ping Pong, owned by Eve C. Olsen.

America as of January 1, 1976, done by Dugan Skinner. The survey showed: Owners, 27; dogs, 56 total; males, 25; bitches, 31. Colors, charcoal and white, 1; cream, 5; white, 1; black and tan, 1; black, 8; fawn, 40. Tails, no tail, 2; stub, 15; medium, 15; medium to long, 9; curled, 15. Coat, extra long, 1; medium, 21; short, 34. Tongues, pink, 7; spotted, 13; black, 35; brown, 1. Temperament, good, 50; not too good, 6. Eyes, problem, 14; no problem, 42.

The fifth organizational meeting of the CSPCA was held on April 23, 1977, at the home of Ernest and Madeline Albright, Pleasant Hill, California. Members present were from California, Oregon, British Columbia, and Indiana. The results of the balloting by Club members showed the election of the following officers: President, Ernest Albright; Vice-President, Walter (Dugan) Skinner; Secretary, Darlene Wright; and Registrar, Dee Seas.

The sixth meeting of the CSPCA was held on June 17, 1978, at Hinckley, Illinois, and may have been one of the most exciting events in the two-thousand-year history of the breed, for it was held in conjunction with the Chinese Shar-Pei Club's first Specialty Show (which was later declared unofficial). This show produced an overwhelming gathering of sixty-three Shar-Pei, with forty-six entered for competition. The total number of dogs was approximately one-third of all Chinese Shar-Pei in America. When we consider the fact that at Hong Kong shows, entries are only a half-dozen or less, we can appreciate the magnitude of the effort made by the CSPCA in furthering the interests of the breed here in America.

Best of Breed at this starting event, which unexpectedly displayed a group of dogs of great overall uniformity in spite of the variations that exist in the breed, was Victor and Dee Seas' homebred Walnut Lane's China Foo. This young dog, whelped May 8, 1975, was sired by Down-Homes Kung Foo (whelped in Macao) out of Down-Homes China Love (whelped in Hong Kong). Both of the parents had been sent to the Seas from Hong Kong by Matgo Law.

Some of the enthusiasm generated by this outstanding event was dampened when it was learned that in the excitement of planning this first Specialty, someone forgot to send official announcements of the meeting to all Club members. Not all members were notified and therefore did not have a chance to voice their opinions on various matters discussed. As a result, in accordance with AKC regulations, the meeting was declared unofficial.

The seventh annual meeting of The Original Chinese Shar-Pei Club of America was held on June 30, 1979, at San Juan Capistrano, California. And the following day (July 1), the 1979 Annual Specialty Show was held in the same city. Sponsored by The Southern California Chinese Shar-Pei Club, with Mrs. Ellen Weathers as Show Chairman, the Specialty was an outstanding success. Mr. Matgo Law of Hong Kong judged, and the show attracted widespread attention, as was evidenced by some seventy entries, including dogs from various sections of the United States as well as some from Canada and Italy.

Placements (including names of owners) were as follows:

Puppy, Dogs, 3 Months and Under 6 Months
1. Wun Sun, Dr. and Mrs. Maier, Fullerton, CA
2. Bedlam's Bandit, J. and A. Weathers, San Juan Capistrano, CA
3. Tunzi's Peregrine Took, Mr. and Mrs. G. Photakis, Burr Ridge, IL
4. Ho Wun II Mr. Pong, Zella Llewellyn, Alvin, TX

Puppy, Dogs, 6 Months and Under 9 Months
1. Sui Yeen's Chin Chu, Mr. and Mrs. M. Stone, Northfield, NJ
2. Sis-Q's Fu Man Chew, J. and B. Small, Norco, CA
3. Down Homes Black Woo Loo, Mr. and Mrs. L. Rafferty, Eagle Creek, OR
4. Chin-I Samarai Sam, Linda Angelo, Quartz Hill, CA

Puppy, Dogs, 9 Months and Under 12 Months
1. Tunzi's Wouki, Susan Tunzi, Petaluma, CA
2. Tunzi's Han Solo of Raintree, Linda Gaetan, Boneto, CA

Dogs, Bred by Exhibitor
1. Sui Yeen's Chin Chu, P. and E. Evert, Northfield, NJ
2. Chin-I Samurai Sam, Linda Angelo, Quartz Hill, CA
3. Tunzi's Wouki, Susan Tunzi, Petaluma, CA
4. Ho Wun II Mr. Pong, Darlene Wright, Concord, CA

Dogs, 1 Year but Under 3 Years
1. Ho Wun Kong, D. Wright, Concord, CA
2. Shir Du Sam Ku, Bedlam Kennels, San Juan Capistrano, CA
3. Down Homes Dark Solo, J. Lorenzen, Aldergrove, BC, Canada
4. Mr. Chan, R. and M. Meggelin, Pleasant Hill, CA

Dogs, 3 Years and Over
None shown.

Dogs, American Bred
1. Eshaf's Hoi-Ti, E. and E. Fahse, Cicero, IL
2. Sis Q's Fu Man Chew, J. and B. Small, Norco, CA
3. Eshaf's Kan Tung, Dawn Walling, Milpitas, CA
4. Siskiyou's Dr. Blue, Lois Alexander, San Luis Obispo, CA

Above, Suzy Que, owned by Robert W. Cook, East Berlin, Pennsylvania.

Above, puppy owned by Linda B. Murphy, Toledo, Ohio.

Below, puppy at Matgo Law's Down-Homes Kennels, Hong Kong, 1978.

Dogs, Foreign Bred
1. Down Homes Cream Woo, Bedlam Kennels, San Juan Capistrano, CA
2. Down Homes Union Jack, Jacquelene De Maiori, Los Angeles, CA
3. Down Homes Black Woo Loo, L. and S. Rafferty, Eagle Creek, OR
4. Down Homes Dark Solo, Jim Lorenzen, BC, Canada

Veteran Stud Dog
1. Shir Du Sam Ku, Bedlam Kennels, San Juan Capistrano, CA
2. Ho Wun II Kong, Darlene Wright, Concord, CA

Puppy, Bitches, 2 Months to 3 Months
1. Eshef's Ai Jen of Bedlam, E. and E. Fahse, Cicero, IL
2. Eshaf's Yu-Shan-Te, E. and E. Fahse, Cicero, IL

Puppy, Bitches, 3 Months but Under 6 Months
1. Bedlam's Night Song, Bedlam Kennels, San Juan Capistrano, CA
2. Ho Wun II Shantung, Darlene Wright, Concord, CA
3. Lady Chan, R. and M. Megglin, Pleasant Hill, CA
4. Chin I Ming Ta-Ma-So, Claudine Mulhein, Riverside, CA

Puppy Bitches, 6 Months and Under 9 Months
1. Cash Chew, J. and B. Small, Norco, CA
2. Ei Ling, Dr. and Mrs. Maier, Fullerton, CA
3. Madame Chew, J. and B. Small, Norco, CA
4. Cho Lin Yang, Jane Zintak, Rome, Italy

Puppy, Bitches, 9 Months and Under 12 Months
1. Bedlam's Liquorish of Jih Lo, Anetta Harris, Chanute, KS
2. Linn's Ping, Zella Llewellyn, Alvin, TX
3. Ho Wun II Yum Yum, Gaynell Wolf, Bailey City, CO
4. Su Chew, J. and B. Small, Norco, CA

Bitches, Bred by Exhibitor
1. Albright's Fawn, E. Albright, Pleasant Hill, CA
2. Ei Long, Dr. and Mrs. Maier, Fullerton, CA
3. Bedlam's Won Pe Ti Hi, Bedlam Kennels, San Juan Capistrano, CA
4. Ho Wun II Shantung, Darlene Wright, Concord, CA

Bitches, 1 Year and Under 3 Years
1. Down Homes Oriental Pearl, Bedlam Kennels, San Juan Capistrano, CA
2. Yuk Lan, June Collins, San Diego, CA
3. Bedlam's Al Jen, Roland A. Fischer, Alexandria, MN
4. Tai Seng, G. Martin, Concord, CA

Bitches, 3 Years and Over
1. Down Homes Little Pea, Lois Alexander, San Luis Obispo, CA
2. Down Homes Happy Ambassador, M. and B. Calltharp, Raytown, MO

Bitches, American Bred
1. Sui Yun Firecracker of Bedlam, Bedlam Kennels, San Juan Capistrano, CA
2. Linn's Ping, Zella Llewellan, Alvin, TX

Bitches, Foreign Bred
1. Down Homes Miss Oscar, Roberta Galloway, Foster City, CA
2. Down Homes Happy Ambassador, M. B. Calltharp, Raytown, MO
3. Tai Seng, G. Martin, Concord, CA

Veteran Bitch
1. Down Homes Little Pea, Lois Alexander, San Luis Obispo, CA

Brood Bitches
1. Down Homes Little Pea, Lois Alexander, San Luis Obispo, CA

Obedience (no scores available)
1. Ho Wun Fawn, E. Albright
2. Linn's Ping, Zella Llewellyn
3. Cash Chew, B. Small

Junior Showmanship
1. Ray Gaetan
2. Dominga Tunzi
3. Jeff Angelo
4. (Name not available)
5. Greg Angelo

Eve Olsen's dog and bitch—showing correct up-tolt of anus.

Fortunately, the confusion over the 1978 Specialty Show has proved to be only a minor event in the life of the CSPCA. As will be seen by the following list of members, current as of September 1979, the CSPCA has continued to grow at an ever-increasing rate.

Mrs. Donna Aiello
5137 Leland
Amarillo, Texas 79110

Ernest and Madeline Albright
Ho Wun Kennels
24 Audrey Lane
Pleasant Hill, California 94523

Lois Alexander
1853 Partridge Drive
San Luis Obispo, California 93401

Beverly Anderson
220 North 32nd
Parsons, Kansas 67357

Ray Anderson
7 Old Dorwart Street
Lancaster, Pennsylvania 17603

Linda Angelo
436 37-N 51 Street West
Quartz Hill, California 93534

Emeline Ashdon
5736 Sattely Lake Road
Mancelona, Michigan 49659

Roma Baker
4121 Briarcrest Road
Toledo, Ohio

Wayne and Charleen Bale
519 East Drayton
Ferndale, Michigan 48220

R. A. Bartha
1650 Alta Dina Place
Atlanta, Georgia 30311

Sylvia Bell
1210 Fifth Street
Moundsville, West-Virginia 26041

Thomas and Nancy Bell
10021 Lazy Oaks
Houston, Texas 77080

Thomas V. Blanton, Jr.
502 Tuckahoe Boulevard
Richmond, Virginia 23226

Jacqueline and Lawrence Bulgin
211 Orleans Court
Columbia, Missouri 65201

Jeanne Burek
6120 West 127th Place
Palos Heights, Illinois 60463

Joan M. Burke
184 Airmount Road
Mahwah, New Jersey 07430

Bob Calltharp
9705 East 80th Street
Raytown, Missouri 64138

Virgil and Karen Carter, Jr.
Route Box 256-13
Corydon, Kentucky 42406

Martha J. Clanton
726 Lake Park Boulevard
Muscatine, Iowa 52761

M. D. Cogburn
Route 10, Box 540
Moore, Oklahoma 73160

June Collins
4430 Arista Drive
San Diego, California 92103

Pat Crawford
1704 Hiawatha NE
Albuquerque, New Mexico 87112

Lawrence Dale or Shirley Long
3207 Embudito Drive NE
Albuquerque, New Mexico 87111

Michael and Donna Dunning
5705 Lindenwood
Saint Louis, Missouri 63109

Brian Ekstrom
470 Three Calgary Place
Calgary, Alberta T2P Q1J
Canada

Jackie and Paul Evert
1604 Wanamassa Drive
Wanamassa, New Jersey 07712

Emil and Vern Fahse
Eshaf Kennels
5101 West 31st Place
Cicero, Illinois 60650

Jean Fein
378 East Loveland Avenue
Loveland, Ohio 45140

Patricia T. Ferdman
7537 Conestoga Way
San Diego, California 92120

Ruth Fink
Box 352, Route 3
Elizabethtown, Pennsylvania 17022

Jean Finney
2058 Polk Avenue
San Mateo, California 94403

Rachel Fischer
Route 7, Box 772
Alexandria, Minnesota 56308

Joan Franson
6804 Dover
Arvada, Colorado 80004

Joyce Fritts
9350 Station Road
Erie, Pennsylvania 16510

Linda Gaeton
5166 Glen View Place
Bonita, California 92002

Mrs. R. Galloway
830 Lurline Drive
Foster City, California 94404

Michael and Elizabeth Gibson
1067 Hosbrook Street
Indianapolis, Indiana 46203

John Grady
1200 Oakhaven Drive
Roswell, Georgia 30075

Bill Gremminger
Gremwood Shepherds
Route 1, Box 84A
Robertsville, Missouri 63072

Jacob and Dolly Groby
Route 1, Box 143
Buna, Texas 77612

Roi P. Guay
8091 Chapman Avenue, Apt. #2
Stanton, California 90680

John A. Hackley
P.O. Box 99237
Tacoma, Washington 98499

Joyce Hanes
6517 Danville Court
Rockville, Maryland 20852

Annetta Harris
P.O. Box 337
Chanute, Kansas 66720

Dr. Jack and Kari Isaacs
3038 Oakraider Drive
Alamo, California 94507

R. E. G. Jackson
Box 265
Linden, Alberta T0M 1J0
Canada

Leo and Lynette Jansen
Route 3
Newton, Illinois 62448

Valerie Krause
911 North Roxbury Drive
Beverly Hills, California 90210

Jane Langdon
507 Central Avenue
Alameda, California 94501

Eleanor Latulippe
2255 Las Amigas Road
Napa, California 94558

Matgo and Harine Law
Down-Homes Kennel
GPO Box 7339 Central
Hong Kong, British Crown Colony

R. A. Lewellyn
Shoestring Acres Kennels
Route 2, Box 285
Alvin, Texas 77511

Dale and Kay Lewis
13104¼ Kornblum
Hawthorn California 90250

Dale Long
3203 Embudito Drive
Albuquerque, New Mexico 87111

Jim Lorenzen
3636 - 254 Street
Aldergrove, British Columbia V0X 1A0
Canada

Conie Lynch
749 San Juis Court
Concord, California 94518

Dr. G. and I. Maier
2700 Madonna Drive
Fullerton, California 92632

Glenn Martin
3907 Juniper Drive
Concord, California 94519

Joyce E. Mayfield
1800 Creed
Wichita, Kansas 67213

Robert Megglin
2072 Sherman Drive
Pleasant Hill, California 94523

William Morison
40 Jennifer Lane
Alamo, California 94507

Claudine Mulhern
2951 Cindy Lane
Hemet, California 92343

C. Murphy
5154 Kearsdale
Toledo, Ohio 43623

Lisselotte S. Offergeld
c/o Oakridge Nursing Home
Griffin and Leon Streets
El Dorado, Arkansas 71730

R. and S. Olnhausen
Box 84, Route 1
Wyncrest Road
Marlboro, New Jersey 07746

Eve C. Olsen
Willowledge Farm
Haywood, Virginia 22722

Judy Orbin
1465 Poplar Street
Flint, Michigan 48503

Pat Pagnard
Route 1
Morral, Ohio 43337

Roy Parker
P.O. Box 59383
Los Angeles, California 90059

James Parks
2772 Shakertowne Road
Xenia, Ohio 45385

Norman Phillip
Box 81
Orleans, California 95556

George Photakis
7700 South County Line Road
Burr Ridge, Illinois 60521

Folke and Darlene Pira
2703 Elmwood
Wichita Falls, Texas 76308

John Piscazzi
1680 Merriman Road
Akron, Ohio 44313

Kirk and Lynn Pollard
2812 Bidwell #2
Davis, California 95616

Larry Rafferty
P.O. Box 73
Eagle Creek, Oregon 97022

Gary Rasor
P.O. Box 429
Royal City, Washington 99357

Thomas and Lois Rice
Boom Road
Saco, Maine 04072

Judy Ritter
2336 Auburn
Northbrook, Illinois 60062

Sherman K. Robbins
P.O. Box 52092
Houston, Texas 77052

Connie Robertson
Star Route
Orick, California 95555

The Reverend Walter and Nancy Rockabrand
21280 Bonanza Boulevard
Elkhorn, Nebraska 68022

Alfred Russell
1020 - 15th Street, #34-A
Denver, Colorado 80202

Steven Russell
2938 North Lakewood
Chicago, Illinois 60657

Jonnie M. Ruth
1026 Cary Memorial
Pensacola, Florida 32505

T. and H. Sawyer
Star Route 2, Box 20
Greenwood, California 95635

Frances Scaife
5201 Westminster Place
Pittsburgh, Pennsylvania 15232

Don and Susan Scheer
5775 Garber Drive NE
Atlanta, Georgia 30328

Mr. and Mrs. M. Schmied
Box 36
Grand Marais, Manitoba R0E 0T0
Canada

Victor and Dee Seas
Route 2, Box 89
182 Whetstone River Road South
Caledonia, Ohio 43314

Gloria Seifman
21 Seward Lane
Stony Brook, New York 11790

Walter and Shirley Skinner
Shir Du Kennels
Box 388
Wolcottville, Indiana 46795

Mr. Jack Small
1425 East Belmont
Ontario, California 92675

W. T. Smith
Apartment 101 Fernwoody Drive
Upper Sandusky, Ohio 43351

C. Spinks
4620 Reka Drive #22
Anchorage, Alaska 99504

Mr. J. M. Stone, Jr.
108 Northwood Court
Northfield, New Jersey 08225

Robert and Ruth Stuart
2535 River Road
Modesto, California 95351

Martha Sullivan
1504 Las Arbobs NW
Albuquerque, New Mexico 87112

Thomas and Shirley Sweet
R.D. 5
Mansfield, Ohio 44903

Linda Teitelbaum
11 Dogwood Lane
Lawrence, New York 11559

Above, Sir Chew, bred by Ellen Weathers and owned by Jack and Bettye Small.

Above, Willowledge Ping Pong, owned by Eve C. Olsen.

Right, Eve Olsen's Chinese Shar-Pei.

Below, Paul Strang with street dog in Macao, 1977.

Below, Down-Homes China Love, bred by Matgo Law and owned by De Jon Seas, Harpster, Ohio.

K. M. Thiede
16201 El Camino Real #28
Houston, Texas 77062

Susan Tunzi
4497 Old Adobe Road
Petaluma, California 94952

James and Nanny Tyler
343 North Glengarry
Birmingham, Michigan 48010

Sonia Z. Urmacher
300 East 56th Street, Apartment 14C
New York, New York 10022

Gloria Valentine
P.O. Box B, Route 23
Stockholm, New Jersey 07460

George Von Borstel
1408 Greenview Way
Lawrenceville, Georgia 30245

Loretta Voss
P.O. Box 251
Smithflat, California 95727

Ng Wah-Chiu
2021 Walter SE
Albuquerque, New Mexico 87102

Mr. and Mrs. R. Walling
883 Russell Lane
Milpitas, California 95035

James Weathers
27341 Ortega Highway
San Juan Capistrano, California 92675

Edwin W. Weaver
703 Cogdell Circle
Webster, New Jersey 14580

Bob and Joanne Webster
12805 Kludge Road
Cypress, Texas 77429

Peter and Molly White
4001 Oakhurst
Amarillo, Texas 79109

Gaynell M. Wolf
Route 1, Box 383
Pine, Colorado 80470

James and Darlene Wright
Ho Wun II Kennels
3207 Sheffield Place
Concord, California 94518

Rudy Yarbrough
2743 Ridgewood Drive
Turner, Oregon 97392

Above, Robert and Sylvanna Chan, Hong Kong.

Above, a Chinese Diamond puppy.

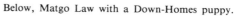

Below, Matgo Law with a Down-Homes puppy.

E. Ted Linn of Asheville, North Carolina, who had assembled an important Shar-Pei kennel comprised of some twenty dogs, many imported from Hong Kong and Taiwan and others purchased from other United States breeders, conceived the idea of an independent Shar-Pei club in 1978. The first public organizational meeting of The Chinese Shar-Pei Club of America, Inc. (East Coast), was held at the Atlanta, Georgia, Airport Ramada Inn on February 10 and 11, 1979, and attracted about twenty breeders and fanciers, who came from the Mid-West and points up and down the East Coast. All showed great enthusiasm in forming a new club, for the surging popularity of the breed had suddenly spawned a great number of new fanciers. The optimism generated during this two-day Atlanta meeting was contagious, and a number of new ideas for projects to further the interests of the breed were formulated.

The following list of members of The Chinese Shar-Pei Club of America, Inc. (East Coast), is correct as of October 10, 1979. From this list we see that some fanciers are members of both this and the original club.

Anita and Beverly Alchin
109 Peter Street
Strathpine 4500
Queensland, Australia

Ray Anderson
7 Old Dorwart Street
Lancaster, Pennsylvania 17603

Mr. and Mrs. Paul Antaya
13 Dartnell Place
Bramalea, Ontario L6T 1P3
Canada

Roma J. Baker
4121 Briarcrest Road
Toledo, Ohio 43623

Carin Ballard
Box 355
Fairview, North Carolina 28730

Robert L. and Bonnie J. Barker
8870 Crosby Lake Road
Clarkston, Michigan 48016

Rhea Bartha
1620 Alta Dena Place
Atlanta, Georgia 30311

May Bernstein
2615 SE Tenth Street
Pompano Beach, Florida 33062

Frank H. and Clariele Blackstock
325 Bunting Drive
Savannah, Georgia 31404

Joyce and Brenda Boone
13 Pickwick Road
Asheville, North Carolina 28803

James and Elizabeth Boughner
2370 Adams Road
Lake Orion, Michigan 48035

Clair Bowman
825 Burdett Avenue
Victoria, British Columbia V8W 1B3
Canada

Judy and Robert Brown, DVM
3360 Jackson Drive
Jackson, Wisconsin 53037

Pamela Burd
P.O. Box F2409
Freeport, G.B.I., Bahamas

Elizabeth A. Burden
Box 526
Locust Valley, New York 11560

Jeanne Burek
6120 West 127th Place
Palos Heights, Illinois 60463

Russell Cannon
Box 347
Bethel, Alaska 99559

Marvin Z. Charney, DVM
2410 University Drive
Sunrise, Florida 33322

June and David Collins
4430 Arista Drive
San Diego, California 92103

Robert Cook
Box 59, Route 2
East Berlin, Pennsylvania 17316

Richard Cotugno
9560 N.W. 25th Court
Sunrise, Florida 33323

Barbara Cratty
1921 Marion-Cardington Road E.
Marion, Ohio 43302

Barbara and Robert Devine, DVM
Route 1, Box 214 B
Bayside, California 95524

W. Phillip Dunn
10910 N.W. 12th Place
Gainesville, Florida 32601

Christine Eveld
5521 South Waverly Way
Tempe, Arizona 85283

James F. and Patricia Eveld
5521 South Wavery Way
Tempe, Arizona 85283

Paul A. and Jackie Evert
1604 N. Wanamassa Drive
Ocean, New Jersey 07712

Elverna and Emil Fahse
5101 West 31st Place
Cicero, Illinois 60650

Ruth Fink
Route 3, Box 352
Elizabethtown, Pennsylvania 17022

Mrs. Jack Finney
2607 Woodrow Street
Greenville, Texas 75401

Roland A. Fischer
Route 7, Box 772
Alexandria, Minnesota 56308

Nancy C. Frank
1020 Bennington Road
Virginia Beach, Virginia 23464

Susan Frank
1020 Bennington Road
Virginia Beach, Virginia 23464

Thomas and Joyce Fritts
9350 Station Road
Erie, Pennsylvania 16510

George S. Goldberg
110 E. 9th Street, Suite 425
Los Angeles, California 90015

Dale and Theresa Gootee
134 Prospect Boulevard
Waterloo, Iowa 50701

Gail A. Gordon
311 Brook Avenue
Toronto, Ontario M5M 2L4
Canada

John P. and Janet L. Grady
1200 Oakhaven Drive
Roswell, Georgia 30075

Bill and JoAnn Gremminger
Route 2, Box 115
Dittmer, Missouri 63023

Mr. and Mrs. Kenneth Halbert
4812 Mockingbird Lane
St. Joseph, Missouri 64506

William Hammon
2963 Churchview Avenue
Pittsburgh, Pennsylvania 15227

Doug Harbison
510 Granada Boulevard
Lake Villa, Illinois 60046

Annetta Harris
P.O. Box 337
Chanute, Kansas 66720

Bill and Ann Hearin
9905 S.W. 125th Avenue
Miami, Florida 33186

Elsa Henderson
82 Loucks Avenue
Los Altos, California 94022

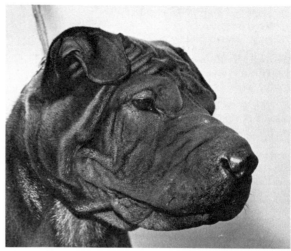

Above, Down-Homes Dark Princess, by Down-Homes King Kong ex Down-Homes Fleur. Breeder, Matgo Law. Owner, Charles Murphy, Jr. Photographer, Ralph Martin.

Above, Foo-Z at four months of age with Cup Cake II on right. Owned by the Walter "Dugan" Skinners, Wolcottville, Indiana.

Below, part of the litter of December 1974 out of Down-Homes Little Pea. Breeder, Lois E. Alexander, San Luis Obispo, California.

Mr. and Mrs. Harold R. Henderson
485 Tremont Street
Duxbury, Massachusetts 02332

Alexander T. Kamwell
427 Hillside Avenue
Orange, New Jersey 07050

Jim and Deloris Kubicek
Route 2
Shawnee, Oklahoma 74801

Barbara E. Kutra
510 Granada Boulevard
Lake Villa, Illinois 60046

Richard S. Lee
3112 W. Orangewood
Phoenix, Arizona 85021

John B. Leonard
32 Saint Lukes Place
Montclair, New Jersey 07042

Dennis and Barbara Lindberg
P.O. Box 1213
Virginia, Minnesota 55792

E. Ted and Annabelle Linn
Route 6, Box 398
Asheville, North Carolina 28730

Richard and Zella Llewellyn
Route 2, Box 285
Alvin, Texas 77511

David Longstaff
P.O. Box 24494
Fort Lauderdale, Florida 33307

Edward W. Lucke, Jr.
Box 356
Mexico Beach, Florida 32410

Charles Massengill, DVM
Route 1
Osceola, Missouri 64776

Frances E. and Hugh F. McIntyre, Jr.
3501 Stoudt's Ferry Bridge Road
Reading, Pennsylvania 19605

Hugh F. McIntyre, III
3501 Stoudt's Ferry Bridge Road
Reading, Pennsylvania 19605

Alice Mendoza
3927 Main Street
East Chicago, Indiana 46312

Craig L. and Amy A. Miller
9241 Ridgetree Drive
Fort Wayne, Indiana 46819

Charles R. and Linda Murphy
5154 Kearsdale Road
Toledo, Ohio 43626

Charles R. Murphy, Jr.
Trever Hall
815 East South Street
Appleton, Wisconsin 54912

Robert and Colleen Myles
2221 Genwa
Dearborn, Michigan 48124

Lowell B. Nesbitt
289 West 12th Street
New York, New York 10014

Bruce Norris
1337 23rd Street N.W.
Canton, Ohio 44709

Dennis and Pat Pagnard
Route 1, County Road 72
Morral, Ohio 43337

Roy Joseph Parker
P.O. Box 59383
Los Angeles, California 90061

Mr. and Mrs. James Parks
315 N. Alpha Bellbrook Road
Xenia, Ohio 45385

John and Margretta Patterson
5124 Riverside Drive
Columbus, Ohio 43220

Michael E. and Janice M. Ping
18623 Indian
Redford, Michigan 48240

John and Nadine Purcell
920 Wilson Road
Ashland, Oregon 97520

Nina Rauscher
450 East 63rd Street
New York, New York 10021

James and Judy Raymond
16761 Helen
Southgate, Michigan 48195

Linda Reinelt
Süshorn 7
2209 Elskop/Süderau
West Germany

Mark and Susan Rhodes
3112 W. Orangewood
Phoenix, Arizona 85021

Steve and Stephanie Rose
1109 Steve Mar Drive
Columbus, Georgia 31904

Patti Schwieterman
5730 Bonsel Parkway
Toledo, Ohio 43615

Victor C. and De-Jon "Dee" Seas
Route 2, Box 89
182 Whetstone River Road So.
Caledonia, Ohio 43314

Gloria Seifman
21 Seward Lane
Stony Brook, New York 11790

George Sladovich III
4828 Fairfield Street
Metaire, Louisiana 70002

Jack and Bettye Small
1425 East Belmont
Ontario, California 91761

Electa Smith
Route 5, Box 12101
Wyandot County Road #110
Upper Sandusky, Ohio 43351

Linda C. Smith
12021 148th Avenue, S.E.
Renton, Washington 98055

Wilma Smith
435½ North Fourth Street
Upper Sandusky, Ohio 43351

Joseph and Rose Ellen Stone
108 Northwood Court
Northfield, New Jersey 08225

Paul D. Strang
1650 33rd Street N.W.
Washington, D.C. 20007

Bart and Marilyn Sullivan
Route 1
Dunlap, Iowa 51529

Mike and Elaine Thompson
6901 Valley View
Jenison, Michigan 49428

Robert and Carolann Treiber
134 N. Timber Lane
Cheshire, Connecticut 06410

Emile Trottier
22 Bertmount Avenue
Toronto, Ontario M4M 2X9
Canada

Mr. and Mrs. George Von Borstal
1408 Greenview Way
Lawrenceville, Georgia 30245

Jim and Ellen Weathers
27341 Ortega Highway
San Juan Capistrano, California 92675

William C. West
76th Army Band
HHC A5G-K
Box 913 APO
New York, New York 09054

Paul Wettlaufer
1550 Avenue Road
Toronto, Ontario M5M 3X5
Canada

Jeff and Barbara Wilcoxson
527 N.E. 56th Street
Miami, Florida 33137

Pamela Zielinger
386 East Eighth Street
South Boston, Massachusetts 02127

Jane Zintak
Piazza di Trevi 100
Rome, Italy 00187

Annabelle (Mrs. E. Ted) Linn, Asheville, North Carolina, with two of the Linns' Shar-Pei.

Chinese Shar-Pei with children, pictured in Taiwan.

Left, Down-Homes Kung Fu, whelped May 28, 1973, by Luck-Son ex Kay-Fay. Breeder, Mr. Y. K. Leung, Macao. Owner, De Jon Seas, Harpster, Ohio.

Below, Walnut Lanes China Foo, whelped May 6, 1975, by Down-Homes King Foo ex Down-Homes China Love. Breeders-owners, Victor and De Jon Seas.

The first organizational meeting of the Southern California Chinese Shar-Pei Club was held at the home of Jack and Bettye Small, Norco, California, on January 20, 1979. Those present besides the Smalls, included Jim and Ellen Weathers, Roy Parker, Linda Gaetan, Jeff and Tricha Jarosz, and Louise Lloyd.

At this meeting it was decided that the Southern California Club would not be an independent organization but instead would constitute an affiliate of The Original Chinese Shar-Pei Club of America. This local chapter, therefore, does not register Shar-Pei but leaves that task to the parent club.

The second meeting of the Southern California Chinese Shar-Pei Club was held at the home of Jim and Ellen Weathers, San Juan Capistrano, California, on February 17, 1979. Twenty people were in attendance. An election was held and the officers elected were: President, Jim Weathers;

Above, Mr. Wong, owned by Ernest W. Albright.

Below, Mui-Chu, bitch, at three years of age. Mr. Albright's first dog from Macao.

Vice-President, Roy Parker; Recording Secretary and Treasurer, Jack Small; Corresponding Secretary, Linda Gaetan; and Show Chairman, Ellen Weathers.

The main order of business, after the election of officers, was to formulate plans for hosting a National Shar-Pei Specialty Show to be held in San Juan Capistrano on Sunday, July 1, 1979. Show Chairman Ellen Weathers named Linda Gaetan and Bettye Small to the Show Committee. It was moved, seconded, and carried that Jim Weathers invite the Hong Kong authority Matgo Law to judge the show. In planning the 1979 National Specialty Show, the Southern California Chinese Shar-Pei Club has show imagination and skill.

Members of the Southern California Chinese Shar-Pei Club as of July 1979, are:

Ernest and Madeline Albright
24 Audrey Lane
Pleasant Hill, California 93534

Lois E. Alexander
1853 Partridge Drive
San Luis Obispo, California 93401

Linda Angelo
42637 N. 51st Street West
Quartz Hill, California 93534

Frank and Mary Atkinson
21030 Hicks Street
Perris, California 92370

David and June Collins
4430 Arista Drive
San Diego, California 92103

Linda Gaetan
5166 Glen View Place
Bonita, California 92202

Jeff and Tricha Jarosz
1942 E. Rowland
West Covina, California 91791

Hugh and Louise Lloyd
13822 Arthur Avenue
Paramount, California 90723

Gottlieb and Irene Maier
2700 Madonna Drive
Fullerton, California 92635

Roy and Jackueline Parker
P.O. Box 59383
Los Angeles, California 90061

Jack and Bettye Small
1425 East Belmont
Ontario, California 91761

James and Ellen Weathers
27341 Ortega Highway
San Juan Capistrano, California 92675

Above, puppy at Matgo Law's kennel in Hong Kong.

Above, Paul Strang with Robert Chan in Hong Kong.

Below, Cash Chew, by Down-Homes Don Don ex Down-Homes Sam Boa. Breeder, Anum Kealamakia. Owners, Jack and Bettye Small, Norco, California.

Below, Matgo Law with Mrs. Jon Patterson, 1978.

Registering Your Chinese Shar-Pei

In order to achieve official AKC recognition for our breed, it is absolutely essential that every Shar-Pei be registered in an official stud book.

With a breed that is already recognized, this is a relatively simple matter. All that is necessary is to fill in the AKC registration application blank with the appropriate information. The names and registration numbers of both sire and dam must, of course, correspond with the pedigree information already on file.

But with a rare new breed, such as the Shar-Pei, information on the dog's ancestry may be incomplete, or, in fact, completely lacking.

Until recently, most of the Shar-Pei in the United States have been registered with The Original Chinese Shar-Pei Club of America.

Persons desiring information regarding registration of a dog with this club should write to: Registrar, The Original Chinese Shar-Pei Club of America, Inc., P.O. Box 6512, Concord, CA 94524.

The Chinese Shar-Pei Club of America, Inc. (East Coast), is planning a stringent registration procedure. For the latest information on their requirements, write to: Mrs. Dee Seas, Registrar, Route 2, Box 89, 182 Whetstone River Road South, Caledonia, Ohio 43314.

The American Dog Breeders Association is another club which, in the 1970s, registered a number of Shar-Pei, but under the name *Chinese Fighting Dogs*. The story of the ADBA registration is fascinating and merits close study, for it deals, so far as is known, with the first Shar-Pei brought to America.

Mr. C. M. Chung (Chung Ching Ming), the well-known Hong Kong dog fancier and breeder, is listed as the breeder of the first of these Chinese Fighting Dogs that were registered with the American Dog Breeders Association. "Herman Smith's Lucky" was the name of that first dog, and his owner was Herman Smith of Fresno, California. This dog was whelped August 14, 1965, and his color is given as red.

According to Mrs. Frank Ferris Secretary (at the time) of the ADBA, East Kingston, New Hampshire, the Chinese Fighting Dog was a completely unknown breed back in those days. No Shar-Pei club was yet in existence, and of course the AKC does not register unrecognized breeds, so, as a courtesy to Herman Smith, the ADBA opened a special Stud Book, Volume I, for the new breed and gave Herman Smith's Lucky the number 001.00, the registration date being October 8, 1970.

Lucky's pedigree shows Blue Mynah of Taileh as his sire and Jones' Chow Chow as his dam. The sire of both Blue Mynah and Chow Chow is Eagles Wing of Taileh, with "no record" shown in the space allotted for each of the respective dams. The Hong Kong Kennel Club registration numbers for these dogs are:

Eagles Wing of Taileh, No. 6740;
Blue Mynah of Taileh, No. 7596;
Jones' Chow Chow, No. 8685 A.

While Herman Smith's Lucky appears to have, at first glance, a rather skimpy pedigree, we do note several interesting items. First, since "Jones" is the prefix of Mr. Chung's kennel in Hong Kong, Mr. Chung emerges as the breeder of the first Shar-Pei registered in America. Second, Dah Let is often given as the name of the village in South China from whence came our breed. "Taileh" could be another phonetization of the Chinese characters that give us Dah Let. And, finally, we should remember that a bitch called Jones' "Chow Chow" was not necessarily a bitch of the breed we call Chow, for Mr. Strang discovered, while in the Orient, that the name "Chow Chow" is sometimes given indiscriminately as a pet name to any breed of dog.

Mr. Chung was also the breeder of four more imported Shar-Pei registered on October 8, 1970, by the ADBA as Chinese Fighting Dogs. These were:

No. 002, Gwennala Pitt's Boby, a brown bitch whelped November 1, 1966, sired by Jones' Keeland, HKKC No. 9927, out of Jones' Jane, HKKC No. 8699;
No. 003, J. C. Smith's Bigoo, a red male whelped March 10, 1966, sired by Jones' Keeland, HKKC No. 9927, out of Jones' Chow Chow, HKKC No. 8685 A;
No. 004, J. C. Smith's Roro, a brown bitch whelped November 26, 1966, sired by Eagles

Wing of Taileh, HKKC No. 6740, out of Jones' Buty, a daughter of Blue Mynah of Taileh, HKKC No. 7596, out of Jones' Chow Chow, HKKC No. 8685 A;

No. 005, Darwin D. Smith's Faigoo, a fawn male whelped March 10, 1966, sired by Jones' Keeland, HKKC No. 9927, out of Jones' Chow Chow, HKKC No. 8685 A.

The American Dog Breeders Association also registered on October 8, 1970, four adult Chinese Fighting Dogs that were the direct offspring of the above-named imports. These were:

No. 006, Gwennala (or Gwenola—the Stud Book shows both spellings) Pitt's bitch Tenchy, whelped May 3, 1968, color red, sired by Herman Smith's Lucky, ADBA No. 001, out of Pitt's Boby, ADBA No. 002;

and the three Chinese Fighting Dogs registered as Litter #1, bred by Darwin D. Smith and whelped June 8, 1969. The sire's name is shown variously as Jone's Fai Goo, Smith's Faigoo, and D. D. Smith's Fai Goo, but the registration number for the sire is given consistently as ADBA No. 005 and the name of the sire's owner as Darwin D. Smith. The dam's name is given as Tenchy, ADBA No. 006. The three dogs in Litter #1 were:

No. 007, Mai Ling, bitch, color not given;

No. 008, Hung Chow, a fawn male;

No. 009, Kan Su, fawn bitch.

A little over a year later, on September 29, 1970, Smith's Kan Su whelped a litter of five puppies sired by Fai Goo, ADBA No. 005. These were registered by the American Dog Breeders Association on January 11, 1971, and the names and numbers given as follows:

No. 010, San Goo, fawn male;

No. 011, Ning Tu, red female;

No. 012, Ho Kang, red male;

No. 013, Polotu, fawn female;

No. 014, Yulin, fawn female.

We find, then, that by January 1971 there were fourteen Shar-Pei in the United States registered as Chinese Fighting Dogs. Questions naturally arise: Were there other importations that were not registered? Were there other litters whelped from the registered dogs that have been lost track of?

And another question comes to mind: Can there have been still other Shar-Pei imports that arrived under still another name?

In considering this question, we should remember that the Chinese Fighting Dog has also been called the Chinese Sharkskin Dog, and that ap-

parently this latter name was also used in the United States in referring to the breed we know today as the Chinese Shar-Pei.

Surely someday, some historian working on the literature dealing with dogs will turn up names, dates, and places spelling out the importation of Shar-Pei into the United States under the name Chinese Sharkskin Dog.

The most important thing to remember, however, about the records we have dealing with the dogs registered in the Stud Book of the American Dog Breeders Association, is that some years before all the publicity broke about the Shar-Pei, giving rise to frenzied activity to secure Shar-Pei from abroad, we already had, here in the United States, a number of fine Shar-Pei. Fortunately for the breed, these American Shar-Pei were discovered and astute breeders such as Ernest Albright, Carl Sanders, Russell Cannon, and Ted Linn were able to incorporate the bloodlines of the original imports bred by Mr. Chung with the bloodlines of the New Shar-Pei being sent to us by Matgo Law.

In studying the registration papers of the dogs sent to us by Mr. Chung and Mr. Law, we notice that while the dogs often had common ancestors going back to Macao bloodlines, the dogs sent by Chung had been registered with the Hong Kong Kennel Club, while those sent by Law were registered with the Hong Kong and Kowloon Kennel Association. The explanation lies in the fact that the dogs from Chung arrived in the 1960s when the only registering body was the Hong Kong Kennel Club. Shortly thereafter, Chung, Law, and others founded the new organization—the Hong Kong and Kowloon Kennel Association. And from that time forward the Hong Kong Kennel Club ceased to register Shar-Pei, so those from Law which came to us in the 1970s were registered with the Hong Kong and Kowloon Kennel Association.

The Hong Kong and Kowloon Kennel Association has been successful from the very beginning. It holds two all-breed championship shows each year—one in the spring and another in the fall. Judges for the shows come from countries around the world: Japan, Australia, the United Kingdom, and the United States. American judges who have officiated there include Mr. Vincent G. Perry, Mr. Isidore Schoenberg, Mr. Dick Beauchamp, Mr. C. L. Savage, and Mr. and Mrs. John B. Patterson.

Entries of Shar-Pei at these shows have been

quite small, usually only a half dozen or so, due, of course, to the rarity of the breed—even in Hong Kong. The big winner is Matgo Law's Down-Homes Clown-Nosed Buddha. This dog has taken Best of Breed and First in the Any Other Variety Group three times under judges Isador Schoenberg, C. L. Savage, and (in 1978) Mrs. John B. Patterson.

Officers of the Hong Kong and Kowloon Kennel Association are: President, Mr. Ramon Young; Chairman, Mr. Wai Kee Shun; Honorary Chairman, Mr. Tsang Chiao Sin; Vice-Chairmen, Mr. Matgo Law and Mr. G. E. G. Kew; Honorary Treasurer, Mr. Chung Ching Ming; and Secretary, Mrs. Wendy Kwok. Both Matgo Law and Chung Ching Ming also serve on the Show Committee and, usually, as ring stewards as well.

The address of the Hong Kong and Kowloon Kennel Association is: Room 1304, Bell House, 13/Fl., Block A, 525, Nathan Road, Kowloon, Hong Kong. In their show catalog they wrote: "The Hong Kong and Kowloon Kennel Association invites the general public to join our association. Our association is government licensed to serve all dog-lovers, to promote interest in dogs, and to advance the study, breeding, exhibiting and maintenance of the purity of thorough-bred dogs. It is a place where anyone interested in dogs can get together to exchange knowledge, and assistance on any matter connected with dogs and their pedigree obtained. For further information please contact us."

This gracious invitation to contact the Hong Kong and Kowloon Kennel Association for any needed help or information is of special interest to American Shar-Pei breeders, for the Association will register litters whelped in America if the sire and dam are on record in their Stud Book in Hong Kong.

Above, Ko-Fu, owned by Kenneth Halbert, Saint Joseph, Missouri.

Below, Ah Dan of Chinese Diamond at four years of age (1978).

Three generations: Blach Chen Chu (dam) in center; Foo-Z (granddaughter) on left; and Ling Fu (son) on right. From the Shir Du Kennels of the Walter "Dugan" Skinners.

Ernest W. Albright with Ming Yun, three-year-old bitch; Mem, three-year-old bitch; Ro Ro II, eleven-month-old male; Fawn, eleven-month-old bitch; and China Soule, four-year-old male.

The Hall of Fame

A great many people have become involved in the life and times of the Chinese Shar-Pei in the last few years and all must share, to some extent, the honor of having brought this breed from the brink of oblivion to its present position of eminence. But among all of these hard-working enthusiasts, three towering figures stand out.

Chung Ching Ming (Mr. C. M. Chung) must be named, for it was this Hong Kong breeder who exported the first registered Shar-Pei to this country. And it was also Mr. Chung who served as guide and mentor to Mr. Matgo Law when he was getting his start with these sandy-coated dogs of South China.

"Jones" is the kennel prefix for Mr. Chung's dogs, and anyone who has studied Shar-Pei pedigrees knows how important his dogs have been in giving us the bloodlines with which we are now working. A study of our older pedigrees also reveals how diligently Mr. Chung must have searched the Macao region in order to discover and retrieve some of the last remaining specimens to be found there. Whenever we see Macao given as the place of origin of one of our Shar-Pei's ancestors, there is good reason to believe that the animal in question was a Chung selection.

But Mr. Chung's career has not been limited to the Shar-Pei alone. Actually, he is one of the outstanding dog fanciers in Hong Kong and is most active in all sorts of activities connected with the dogs there. He serves as Honorary Treasurer for the Hong Kong and Kowloon Kennel Association and helps their Show Committee. And in addition to Shar-Pei he is involved with a number of other breeds, including French Bulldogs, Pointers, Rottweilers, Doberman Pinschers, Chows, and Dalmatians. Some of his young sons and daughters also show and breed dogs. But it is as a Shar-Pei fancier that the American breeders cannot afford to forget Mr. Chung.

Matgo Law is the second of our Hall of Fame preeminent personalities. And this is the man most of us regard as "Mr. Shar-Pei," himself. After all, it was his letter, published in the United States in April 1973, in which he appealed for help from the outside world to save the Shar-Pei from extinction, that aroused such far-flung interest in the breed.

The first impression of most visitors upon meeting Matgo Law for the first time is one of surprise at his youth. Few American breeders, certainly, are able to gain international fame for their activities while still in their early thirties. But in spite of his youth one quickly realizes, in discussing the dogs, that this man's fame does not rest on a quirk of fate but, in fact, that he knows the breed very well indeed.

Matgo Law and his equally young wife, Harine, live with their infant son in a picturesque tile-roofed villa across the bay from Hong Kong, about thirty miles away from Hong Kong proper. Here, surrounded as far as the eye can see by the local market gardeners' fields of Chinese cabbage, beans, and other green vegetables, is where his famous Down-Homes Shar-Pei Kennel is located.

During Mr. Strang's visit to Hong Kong, he noticed, upon entering the Laws' home, that a bitch with a newly whelped litter of Shar-Pei puppies had been given a place of honor in a corner of the living room—and he was struck by the discovery that dog-lovers around the world are just alike: Nothing is too good for a mother and her new offspring!

When it comes to breeding Shar-Pei, Matgo Law's record is unequaled, and there is hardly a pedigree in the United States that does not carry one or more dogs with the Down-Homes prefix.

Matgo Law judged in America at the National Specialty Show hosted by the Southern California Chinese Shar-Pei Club on July 1, 1979. Fanciers from across the country came to watch this remarkable young man in action and to meet him in person.

Ernest W. Albright is the third figure in our Hall of Fame. This California fancier's success on behalf of the breed has been so extraordinary that we decided to let him tell the story in his own words. And so, in a letter dated February 25, 1979, he wrote as follows:

"Here is my story: (My wife Madeline has helped in all my endeavors.)

"Several years before my retirement in 1968 I started looking around for a good hobby and decided to breed dogs—dogs that would be especially good for the protection of retired people.

"After looking at a number of rare breeds, I

decided I wanted a breed that would weigh about fifty pounds and finally decided on the Shar-Pei.

"In April 1973 I contacted Matgo Law and he sent me Mui Chu, a bitch that had been bred in Macao. A few weeks after her arrival, she became ill and was successfully treated at the University of California Veterinary School in Davis. She had been bred before leaving Hong Kong but did not whelp her litter. Mui Chu was about eighteen inches tall, weighed about fifty pounds, and was fawn-colored with very short, harsh coat. She was very powerful and her tongue, gums, and the roof of her mouth were all very dark blue.

"Mui Chu was probably the first Shar-Pei ever exhibited in the United States, for she was shown in December 1973.

"In January 1974, I got my second dog from Matgo Law. This was Down-Homes China Souel (Chin). During 1974 I took Chin through obedience school in a very short time. He completed Novice A off-leash.

"In 1974 Chin sired five puppies out of Mui Chu but only three survived.

"In 1974 I obtained three (Arizona-bred) dogs from J. C. Smith. These were Gwei Loh (Foreign Devil), So So, and Ho Ho. The sire and dam of these dogs had been registered with the Hong Kong Kennel Club in 1966. Gwei Loh has sired almost all blue-tongued puppies. I bred Chin to So So and they produced Ling Ling, whose photo appeared on the cover of *Dog Fancy* magazine.

"Ling Ling's picture was taken by Ozzie Sweet of Frances Town, New Hampshire. Other photos that he took at this time appeared around the world. I got letters from New Zealand, Australia, and all over the world. Since then my aim has been to get good photos, expose the intelligence of these dogs, and make contact with the right public relations people who could help promote the dogs.

"As a result, here are some of the places my dogs have been seen: The CBS show *To Tell the Truth,* with Gary Moore; the AKC headquarters in New York, where Mr. Stifel [the President of the AKC] had pictures taken; the David Frost national program in Las Vegas; and on almost every Canadian TV station. I was also interviewed on many Canadian radio stations. At the Metropolitan in Toronto, our Shar-Pei, Ro Ro II, a male, and Tara and Ting, both bitches, were benched next to "Kirk," a dog owned by William Shattner of Star Trek [the popular American motion picture and television production], but the Shar-Pei drew the bigger crowd, by far. In fact, attendance at the show was the biggest they had ever had.

"The movie *The Billion Dollar Hobo,* starring Tim Conway and Will Geer, also starred our three-month-old Tara. In the movie she was called "Li Chien Wu." A paperback book, based on this movie, has been published with pictures of Tara.

"Other pictures of my dogs have appeared in *Popular Dogs,* 1973; in *Dogs Magazine,* April 1974; and in *Dog Fancy* magazine four times. Also in *The National Enquirer; The Star Weekly; The New York Times; The Washington Post;* and hundreds of other newspapers around the world. As a result of all this publicity, we receive, constantly, letters and phone calls from around the globe. And besides all this, our dogs are in the *Guinness Book of World Records.*"

From the above, it is easy to understand why, whenever and wherever the Shar-Pei is mentioned, the name of Ernest Albright is sure to follow.

Linn's Ti I Nan Hai, cream male whelped January 28, 1978, by Down-Homes Man Sang ex Albright's Choo Moo. Breeder-owner, E. Ted Linn, Asheville, North Carolina.

Chinese Shar-Pei in Taiwan.

Right, Robert Chan's bitch in Hong Kong, 1977. Note heavy wrinkles and lack of tail.

Left, Fu Man Chew at four months of age. By Shir-Du Sam Ku ex Down-Homes Little Pea. Breeder, Lois E. Alexander. Owners, Jack and Bettye Small, House of Chew, Norco, California.

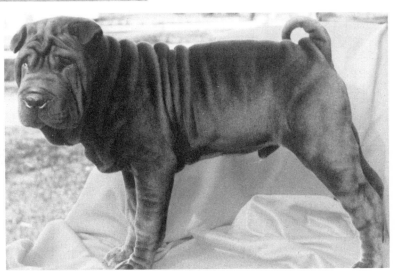

Right, Robert Chan's stud dog. Hong Kong, 1977.

The Future of the Breed

The Shar-Pei's resounding success here in America has not gone unnoticed in other countries. Our American Chinese Shar-Pei Clubs now include members from Canada and Italy, and American breeders report inquiries from England, France, and Germany.

Pictures and articles on the breed have appeared in newspapers and periodicals around the world. Reports have been received claiming the existence of scattered specimens of the breed in Japan, Korea, North Vietnam, and even in faraway Manchuria.

Tass, the chief news agency of the Soviet Union, promised that a pair of the dogs would appear in 1979 at the popular International Exhibition at Brno, Czechoslovakia, behind the Iron Curtain.

Our first reaction, on viewing all this activity on behalf of a breed so recently reported as nearly extinct, is to marvel at this dog's prodigious success in overcoming the odds against his survival, but there is still another interesting aspect to the story.

Hong Kong, because of the dedication of Shar-Pei breeders there, has become a mecca for breeders everywhere, and more and more fanciers are converging on this city in order to obtain first-hand information on the dogs.

Sometimes overlooked by vacationing travelers who thought of it mainly as a business and financial outpost of the British Empire, Hong Kong is now being discovered by these pilgrims to be one of the truly great garden-spot vacation places of our modern world. Of course there are skyscrapers, luxury hotels, and traffic-congested freeways, but there are also the magnificent semitropical South China Sea harbors with yachts, great steamers, jet-propelled hydroplanes, and brightly painted Chinese junks, either moored or crisscrossing each others' paths, as far as the eye can see out on the bright blue water.

Tucked away around the islands are undiscovered tree-shaded tropical beaches. The people are beautiful and the endless array of restaurants offer an unbelievable variety of dishes that turn every meal into a banquet.

Our wrinkled Shar-Pei, it turns out, has a rather devious aspect in his character. Starting out as an all-purpose companion to the farmers of the Han Dynasty, some two-thousand years ago, he has now transformed himself into an Ambassador of Good Will between the people of Hong Kong and the dog fanciers of the West. He has contrived a brilliant future not only for himself but for the rest of us as well.

Mo-Chu, owned by Kenneth Halbert, Saint Joseph, Missouri.

Ro-Geans Ming Loy of Wyloway at three weeks of age. Owned by Ruth Fink, Elizabethtown, Pennsylvania.